THIMBLEBERRIES®

Classic Country
Expanded Edition

by
Lynette Jensen

Four Seasons of Quilting,
Decorating, and Entertaining Inspirations

This book was designed, produced, and published by Landauer Books
A division of Landauer Corporation
12251 Maffitt Road, Cumming, Iowa 50061

President: Jeramy Lanigan Landauer
Editor-in-Chief: Becky Johnston
Art Director: Laurel Albright
Creative Director: Lynette Jensen
Photographers: Craig Anderson, Amy Cooper, and Dennis Kennedy
Photostyling: Lynette Jensen and Margaret Sindelar
Technical Writer: Sue Bahr
Graphic Technician: DeWayne Studer
Technical Illustrators: Lisa Kirchoff, Linda Bender, and Marcia Cameron

We also wish to thank the support staff of the Thimbleberries® Design Studio:
Sherry Husske, Virginia Brodd, Renae Ashwill, Ardelle Paulson, Kathy Lobeck, Carla Plowman,
Julie Jergens, Pearl Baysinger, Tracy Schrantz, Leone Rusch, Julie Borg, Clarine Howe and Ellen Carter.

This book is printed on acid-free paper.

ISBN: 1-890621-70-6

Printed in China 10 9 8 7 6 5 4 3 2 1

Library of Congress Cataloging-in-Publication Data available on request.

FOREWORD

Much of my success as a designer stems from a desire to create a home filled with calm, quiet, and comfort—but most of all love. For many years I've focused my creative energies on making my family the center of our home. Along the way I've had the privilege of being a source of inspiration for many others seeking the same satisfaction gained from making a house a home.

In this expanded new edition of *Classic Country* you'll find more pages, more quilts, more projects, and more ideas. Added inspirations are drawn from other popular Thimbleberries® books including *Classic Country Christmas, Christmas Cottage, Cottage Comfort,* and *Autumn Accents.*

It is my sincere hope that through the pages of this revised edition you'll discover how easy it is to celebrate the seasons with simple country accents for every room of your house. After all, what can be more rewarding than sharing many of your favorite things with all of your favorite people? If making harmony the heart of your home is as important to you as it is to me, then *Classic Country* is meant just for you.

Lynette Jensen

Contents

INTRODUCTION

For best-selling quilting author and fabric designer, Lynette Jensen, all the comforts of home are found in this lovingly restored two-story Colonial she shares with her husband Neil and two grown children, Matthew, Kerry and husband Trevor, who visit often.

Through the pages of this book, Lynette shares her secrets for successful classic country decorating through a personal tour of her home and gardens. She will show you how to quickly mix and match colors, blend decorating styles, and highlight favorite family pieces through a simple planning process that takes you from basic to beautiful in a matter of minutes.

Discover how easy it is to create a sense of well-being throughout your home with four seasons of classic country decorating themes inspired by designer and teacher Lynette Jensen's unique gift for making harmony the heart of the home.

Collecting

Lynette's passion for collecting began when she couldn't bear to see precious pieces of the past tossed out to make room for the new. Since beauty is in the eye of the beholder, it wasn't long before other people's trash became her treasures.

As a frequent flyer through neighborhood garage sales and antique shops, Lynette collected other people's castoffs, many of which have now become collectibles in their own right.

Featured below are paper and fabric quilt patterns in miniature or scraps of vintage textiles such as a crazy quilt in a variety of antique frames. Cross-stitched samplers or crewel embroidery all depicting a similar theme are grouped for greater impact. Fragile antique paper items such as vintage paper dolls can be a challenge to preserve and display—framing easily solves the problem.

Quilting

The transition from salvaging scraps of vintage textiles and tattered quilts to collecting quality heirlooms was gradual, but became more affordable when Lynette's husband completed law school at the University of Minnesota. After Neil's graduation, they settled in his hometown of Hutchinson, Minnesota, to establish the law practice which he still maintains. Lynette found herself busy with two small children, yet eager to fulfill her creative interests. One day quite by accident she attended a show in a nearby rural community featuring a wonderful display of quilts and antiques gathered by a local quilt collector.

Lynette can still recall thinking to herself, "This is exactly what I want to do."

Soon Lynette was not only collecting quilts, but making them for every room of her house.

Whether antique or recently handcrafted, Lynette finds creative ways to display every new addition to her ever-growing collection of quilts. For a great mix of colors in almost any room, quilts are folded and tucked everywhere— in cupboards and on shelves, in a large antique box from a fish market; in a small wooden tool caddy; and in a much larger old wooden tool box parked on a bench housing even more quilts and comforters.

Designing Fabric

Expressing her creativity through quilting, Lynette discovered that by designing her own line of coordinating prints, solids, and plaids she could get exactly what she needed for her growing collection of pieced patchwork. A licensing agreement signed with RJR Fabrics in 1993 has resulted in an ever-growing line of fabrics anchored by her signature Paintbox Collection.

Known and respected through the quilting world for her Thimbleberries® line of fabrics, Lynette has created an enduring collection of coordinates in a rich palette of country colors that literally spans the seasons. Lynette combines traditional quilt patterns with an appealing array of appliquéd vines, berries, and blossoms. The result is a charming blend of blocks and borders with soft touches of country color for a unique style reminiscent of America's more tranquil past.

Lynette's fabric designs have so much appeal that her design studio located in downtown Hutchinson, in a 100-year-old building with original tin ceilings and hardwood floors has become a destination for Thimbleberries® enthusiasts who visit from around the world. Main Street Cotton Shop, an independent full-service quilting shop located in the Thimbleberries® building, currently stocks the entire line of Thimbleberries® patterns, books, fabrics, and quilts.

For Lynette, a Minnesota native and graduate of the University of Minnesota in Home Economics, the Thimbleberries® design studio and office is a short walk from her home. The spacious studio, filled with antiques and quilts on display, is a wonderful, open, bright spot from which to work and create each day.

Living a Dream

For Lynette, the true joy of her business is that designing quilts and fabric involves doing exactly what she would choose to do for a hobby.

Thimbleberries® was started in 1989 with the introduction of four quilt patterns and now features more than 100 softcover books and patterns, as well as 3 hardcover books published by Rodale Press and 7 hardcover books published by Landauer Corporation.

Thimbleberries® also offers regular new fabric collections, block-of-the month quilt patterns, and a popular club conducted by quilt shops internationally.

Lynette has been a featured guest on television quilting programs and featured in leading publications such as *American Patchwork & Quilting* and *McCall's Quilting*.

Thimbleberries® exhibits Lynette's new collections throughout the year at the International Quilt Market. Lynette also conducts workshops and lectures both nationally and internationally.

However, her home and heart are solidly in Hutchinson, Minnesota, where she can share her enthusiasm for classic country decorating with family, friends, and business associates alike.

Spring

Summer

Harvest

Holiday

OVERVIEW

With today's lifestyles calling for home decorating ideas,
you can make your house a home with special,
personal touches. As you greet each new season
of the year, treat your family and friends to four seasons
of fresh new lifestyle, decorating, entertaining and
quilting inspirations from Lynette Jensen.

On the following pages, you'll find a chapter devoted
to each season—spring, summer, harvest, and holiday—
filled with recipes, ideas, and projects for surface design,
home decor, woodpainting, stenciling, and fun with fabric.
Step-by-step how-tos, illustrations, and full-size patterns,
along with a complete guide to materials and sources,
provide a hands-on guide to creating it yourself.

Lynette has also included a special section of
"swatches to go"—coordinating fabrics selected especially
for each season that blend perfectly to transition you through
the year in style. Thanks to Lynette, you can make it
beautiful and make it easy, too. From decorating to entertaining,
Lynette Jensen offers you the best of everything for creating
four seasons of your own authentic country lifestyle.

Spring Haven

"For me, spring is the first season of the year— filled with new beginnings and the promise of even greater things to come."

For Lynette, spring is the first season of the year and, the garage is a popular room of the house. With her yard and garden, it occurred to Lynette that on a daily basis she saw more of her garage than she did many of the rooms of her house.

Determined to make the garage a place of welcome, Lynette cleaned out all the clutter and painted the walls. Using a combination of several commercial stencils, Lynette topped each wall with a floral stenciled border which immediately lifted the mood to make the garage more cheery than dreary.

Lynette then created a convenient potting center by filling a corner of the garage with an old jelly cupboard crowned with a gate from her grandmother's garden. Other keepsakes that bring back happy memories include the well-worn garden hat and sprinkling can that belonged to her grandmother along with the washboard and garden spade used so often by her mother.

In creating the potting center, Lynette found it unnecessary to replace the glass in the doors of the jelly cupboard because none of the contents—a hodgepodge of ceramic pots, pails, and pans—needed to be kept dust-free. With her assorted garden tools handy, Lynette finds it easy to "think spring" even during Minnesota's harsh winters. Everything she needs to get a head start on seedlings for planting her spring haven is gathered in a memory-filled corner of her garage—a unique "welcome home" center!

19

Garden Journal

*While working with my daughter Kerry and her husband Trevor in planning their garden, I decided
to begin keeping a journal of plans and progress. I also included a plant schematic and
listing of the plants with notations for care after planting. Adding "before and after" photographs and
decorative accents makes this personalized keepsake hardworking but handsome.*

Garden Journal

Step 1   Make this a workbook as well as a
scrapbook. Use it as a way to stay in
touch with your garden, learning as
you go.

Step 2   Begin by making or purchasing a
blank scrapbook. Use acid-free
decorative papers, stickers, and pressed
flowers for accents.

Step 3   Take "before and after" photographs of your
garden in progress and use acid-free tape to
secure them to the pages.

Step 4   Finish with ribbon ties glued to the insides
of the front and back covers, if desired.

low maintenance
Living Wreath

Our family was first treated to a living wreath by our neighbor's 15-year-old daughter, Mary. The wreath is shown in full, above, and in its earliest stage on the opposite page. Planted with chicks and hens and a variety of sedum nestled in sphagnum moss, the wreath filled in throughout the summer. It also served as a candle ring around a glass chimney resting on a large terra cotta saucer on our patio table.

All supplies are available from hobby, craft or garden stores.

Wire Wreath Form

Potting Soil

18 Gauge Wire

Sphagnum Moss

Assorted Sedum Plants

Living Wreath

Step 1 Lay sphagnum moss under wire frame. Moss should be wide enought to pull up and wrap around wire frame.

Step 2 Fill frame with potting soil.

Step 3 Bring moss up and around wire frame holding in soil.

Step 4 Wrap wire around frame holding in soil.

Step 5 Water wreath thouroughly.

Step 6 Poke a small hole in moss and soil and insert plants carefully.

Step 7 Press soil firmly around roots to hold plants in place.

Most sedum are succulent or semi-succulent plant types, so water only as needed, and enjoy your living wreath month after month.

Lynette welcomes spring with painted wooden eggs guaranteed to last the season. With help from her daughter, Kerry, Lynette colors eggs in anticipation of Sunday morning brunch.

Papier-maché bunnies from flea markets can tote more than candy. Beginning in early spring, Lynette fills them with fresh flowers or with painted eggs nestled on Easter basket grass.

Spring is often a season of small beginnings with big results. Lynette challenged members of her quilt guild by giving each a pattern and a bag of fabric scraps. One of the resulting quilts was The Homespun Stars wall quilt shown here. It was so stunning Lynette had to have it!

Lynette's "Beaner" Bunnies greet spring in vests made from fabric scraps. Here, quilts in glorious shades of pastels are like a field of spring flowers bursting into bloom.

Beaner Bunnies

FABRICS & SUPPLIES

10 x 15-inch bonded cotton batting or
any tightly woven fabric such as cotton
calicoes, fine wools, etc. for body

4 x 5-inch scrap of fabric for vest

4 x 5-inch fusible web

1 skein embroidery floss for bunny details; eyes,
nose, whiskers, buttons, etc.

1 skein #8 perle cotton or embroidery
floss for buttonhole-edge stitching

3/4 cup dried navy beans

Optional: a decorative button
for flower on vest

Construction

Step 1   Trace bunny and vest patterns onto template material or paper.

Step 2   Carefully cut out (2) bunny shapes: (1) front and (1) back.

Step 3   Transfer markings onto bunny front for ears, eyes, nose, whiskers, buttons and shirt (the "v's" above and below button markings).

Step 4   Iron 4 x 5-inch piece of fusible web onto vest fabric following manufacturer's instructions. Place vest pattern face down on paper side of prepared fabric and trace (1) vest piece. Flip pattern piece and trace (1) vest piece face up. This will give you a right and left vest piece. Cut and remove paper. Position vest pieces on bunny front. Press in place. Using a buttonhole stitch and either floss or perle cotton, stitch vest to bunny at cuff, neck, front, and bottom of vest.

Step 5   Sew button on vest with stem and leaf detail using an outline/stem stitch and 3 strands of floss. Stitch details of bunny front using an outline/stem stitch and 3 strands of floss, stitch the ear detail and shirt markings.

Step 6   With 3 strands of floss, satin-stitch the nose.

Step 7   With 3 strands of floss, stitch 2 French Knots for eyes.

Step 8   With 3 strands of floss, straight-stitch the whiskers and small "x's" for buttons.

Step 9　With wrong sides together, pin outer edges of bunny together. Start stitching near the bottom and stitch around outside edge with a nice even buttonhole stitch about 1/8-inch deep.

Leave a small opening at bottom, add beans and continue stitching to complete. "Beaner" will plop down anywhere and look right at home.

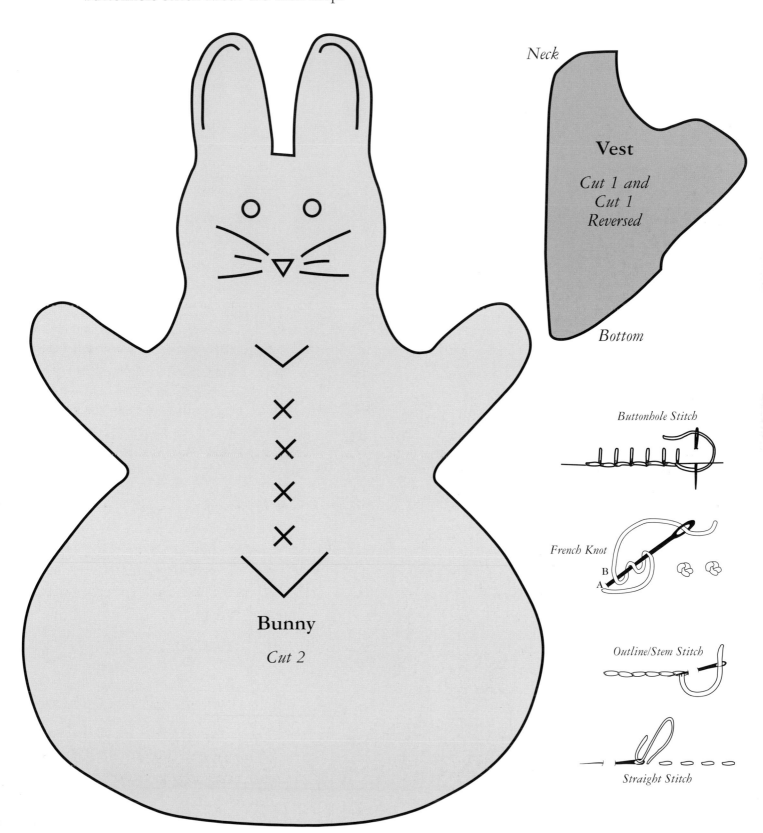

Neck

Vest

Cut 1 and Cut 1 Reversed

Bottom

Bunny

Cut 2

Buttonhole Stitch

French Knot

B

A

Outline/Stem Stitch

Straight Stitch

In the spring, rabbits have a way of multiplying rapidly—almost as fast as Lynette's ever-growing collection of those same charming creatures!

Filling every nook and cranny is always a collector's dream, and Lynette found the challenge of the typical "too narrow to do anything with" space at the top of the stairs just that. She discovered that an antique child's cupboard was just the right size and width to fill the space, but not block the entrance to the adjoining bedroom. Resisting the temptation to give the cupboard a spring spruce up, Lynette left the original paint

and bunny decals. Previously referred to as "peeling paint," now those same features are quite popular in their own right. Crackle glazes and finishes are purposely added to new pieces to make them look old and weathered.

As part of her decorating philosophy, Lynette Jensen is convinced that "what goes around comes around,"

and is content to just let old pieces "be."

Faded papier-maché bunnies from one era seem right at home with collectible pastel pottery flower pots and antique vases.

To create a charming spring decorating theme, Lynette finds it best to group lots of one kind of accessory like the bunnies shown here. She ties them all together with a unifying theme such as the wooden, papier-maché, and candy eggs scattered about just as if the Easter Bunny had already come and gone early on a Sunday morning!

Many of Lynette's quilt designs
are a continuing tribute to her
love for flower beds filled with
spring flowers.

In this small guest bedroom,
more of Lynette's love for
spring's new beginnings
is evident in the embroidered
chicks soaking up the sun
on the blocks featured in
her Flowers in Bloom
quilt and matching
Baby Chicks pillow.

The guest room shown here and on the previous pages is bursting with flowers—from framed to fresh! Blending the old with the new is Lynette's specialty. Her childhood tea set nestled in the tiny cupboard tops off a collection of other favorite toys kept and waiting for playtime to begin.

This antique block was carefully saved from Neil's parents' wedding quilt and preserved under glass.

In the living room shown here, sage sets the stage for Lynette's style of country decorating. This enduring shade of green is mellow, rich, and restful and coordinates with almost all other colors. With sage lending depth and character to the walls, colorful accents of yellow and cream warmed up with splashes of red share the scene.

In the corner, a screen made from discarded shutters removed from Lynette and Neil's home during a renovation nine years ago, provides a textured backdrop for a display of quilt and collectibles. And in the foreground, an old painted pine table serves as a coffee table and nesting place for children's library chairs.

Log Cabin Quilt

FABRICS & SUPPLIES

Finished Size: 72 x 88-inches

Yardage is based on 42-inch wide fabric

5/8 yard **RED PRINT** for center squares

3/8 yard each of 12 **ASSORTED DARK PRINTS** for Log Cabin strips

5/8 yard each of 6 **ASSORTED BEIGE to GOLD PRINTS** for Log Cabin strips

3/4 yard **RED PRINT** for binding

5-1/4 yards **BACKING FABRIC**

Quilt batting, at least 76 x 94-inches

Log Cabin Blocks

Make 99 Blocks

Cutting

From **RED PRINT**:
- Cut 7, 2-1/2 x 42-inch strips. From these strips cut: 99, 2-1/2-inch center squares.

From each of the 12 **ASSORTED DARK PRINTS**:
- Cut 7, 1-1/2 x 42-inch strips.

From each of the 6 **ASSORTED BEIGE/GOLD PRINTS**:
- Cut 13, 1-1/2 x 42-inch strips.

Piecing

*Note: You may vary the position of the **BEIGE/GOLD PRINT** fabrics from block to block, or place them in the same position in each block. The same is true of the **ASSORTED DARK PRINT** fabrics. The fabrics in the quilt shown were varied to create a scrappy look.*

Step 1   Sew a 1-1/2-inch wide **BEIGE/GOLD PRINT** strip to a 2-1/2-inch **RED PRINT** square. Press the seam allowance toward the strip. Trim the strip even with the edges of the center square, creating a two-piece unit.

Trim

Step 2   Turn the two-piece unit a quarter turn to the left. Stitch a different 1-1/2-inch wide **BEIGE/GOLD PRINT** strip to the two-piece unit. Press and trim the strip even with the edges of the two-piece unit.

Trim

Step 3   Turn the unit a quarter turn to the left. Stitch a 1-1/2-inch wide **DARK PRINT** strip to the unit. Press and trim the strip even with the edges of the unit.

Trim

Step 4   Turn the unit a quarter turn to the left. Stitch a different 1-1/2-inch wide **DARK PRINT** strip to the unit. Press and trim the strip even with the edges of the unit.

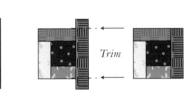

Trim

Step 5   Referring to the block diagram, continue adding 1-1/2-inch wide strips, alternating **BEIGE/GOLD PRINT** strips and **DARK PRINT** strips to complete the Log Cabin block. Press each seam allowance toward the strip just added, and trim each strip before adding the next. Each Log Cabin block should measure 8-1/2-inches square when completed. Adjust the seam allowances if needed.

Make 99

Step 6   Repeat Steps 1 through 5 to make a total of 99 Log Cabin blocks.

Quilt Center

Step 1   Referring to the quilt diagram for placement, sew the Log Cabin blocks together in 11 rows of 9 blocks each. Press the seam allowances in alternating directions by rows so the seams will fit snugly together with less bulk.

Step 2   Pin the rows at the block intersections, and sew the rows together. Press the seam allowances in one direction.

Putting It All Together

Cut the 5-1/4 yard length of **BACKING FABRIC** in half crosswise to form 2, 2-5/8 yard lengths. Refer to Finishing the Quilt on page 203 for complete instructions.

Binding

Cutting

From **RED PRINT**:
- Cut 9, 2-3/4 x 42-inch strips.

Sew the binding to the quilt using a 3/8-inch seam allowance. This measurement will produce a 1/2-inch wide finished double binding. Refer to page 203 for Binding and Diagonal Piecing Instructions.

Log Cabin Quilt

great for dried floral displays
Decoupaged Tins

Vintage postcards and old tins team up with dried flowers from the garden for rustic country-cottage style table top displays. The large tin shown above was my grandmother's seed tin. I first made color copies of cards from my collection, and then decoupaged them to the tin in a random fashion. On the following pages you'll find more than a dozen of my favorite vintage postcards. You're welcome to photocopy them for your personal use only.

SUPPLIES

Rustic or Galvanized Tins

Latex Wall Paint (optional)

Modge Podge Glue®

Vintage Postcards or
Photocopied Reproductions
from the following pages

Decoupage

Step 1   Leave the tin in its natural state or paint it with any
color latex paint you like. Let dry or 4 hours.

Step 2   Trim copies of vintage postcards as desired.

Step 3   Cover the tin with Modge Podge Glue®. While the
glue is still wet, position the cut-out shapes on the tin.
Work in areas, applying Modge Podge Glue® as you
go. Let dry for 4 hours.

Step 4   To seal the surface of the tin, cover the tin once again
with Modge Podge Glue®. Let dry for 4 hours.

Use reproductions of your

own vintage cards, or

simply photocopy

the cards from Lynette's

personal collection

featured on the following

pages. An old sap bucket

such as this works well

for decoupage.

43

The vintage postcards on these two pages are from Lynette's personal collection.
Permission is granted to photocopy for your personal use only.

Greetings on Your
Birthday

May winds blow fair
and skies be blue
And every day bring
joy to you

Birthday Greetings

A Happy Birthday

The vintage postcards on these two pages are from Lynette's personal collection.
Permission is granted to photocopy for your personal use only.

The vintage postcards on these two pages are from Lynette's personal collection.
Permission is granted to photocopy for your personal use only.

forever in bloom
Potpourri

Flowers from the cottage garden will be forever in bloom when you fill a basket or bowl with potpourri. Deadheading all blossoms throughout the summer will give an abundance of petals as well as make the plants thrive. Let the petals dry on newspaper away from humidity and bright sunlight before adding them to the potpourri mix.

Drying flowers

Step 1   Pick flowers at their freshest.

Step 2   For bouquets, tie stems of blossoms together and hang upside down to dry away from humidity and bright sunlight.

Step 3   For individual blossoms, spread them out and allow to dry on newspapers. For potpourri, simply drop any deadheaded blooms into the container and allow to dry and add fragrance to the mix.

Although it requires more time and effort, you can use silica to dry flowers, especially more complex blooms. Silica can be bought at most hobby and craft stores, and some florists. Follow manufacturer's instructions for drying.

Variety is the spice of life. Finding an unusual container for an interesting potpourri mix is only limited by your imagination. Here a wooden bowl fills up quickly with dry leaves and a single hydrangea blossom added for texture.

A tiny spare bedroom can still seem spacious even when filled to the brim. Lynette started the pieced and stenciled May Basket Quilt 16 years ago and finished it as a special housewarming gift for her daughter, Kerry, and son-in-law, Trevor.

Stenciled muslin borders frame the quilt center. The walls are stenciled using a lighter shade of paint for the vertical rows of stenciled floral stripes.

For the windows, ticking-striped fabric valances top off vintage lace curtains for an unfussy touch of softness.

Even though the room is reserved for guests, the small closet was a storage challenge. Solving the problem was a cinch with an old kitchen cupboard painted yellow and stenciled with floral accents. It holds extra quilts and linens, and offers plenty of space for storing guest essentials such a towels, scented soaps, and bath oils.

The trellis and dried florals in a postcard-trimmed galvanized tin repeat the room's garden theme. Lynette used an antique seed tin passed down from her grandmother to display dried florals. The tin has been decorated with antique post-cards (see page 42) and serves with the trellis to enhance the room's garden theme.

Vintage embroidery and crochet pair up in ruffled pillows for the bed. Several years ago, Lynette found the crocheted basket that her grandmother had started but never finished. She turned it into a project by combining it with scraps of embroidery resulting in a pillow for her daughter's home that holds a basket-full of memories!

May Basket Quilt

FABRICS & SUPPLIES

Finished Size: 60 x 88-inches

Yardage is based on 42-inch wide fabric

5/8 yard **ROSE PRINT** for baskets

5/8 yard **GREEN PRINT** #1 for baskets

2-1/3 yards **MUSLIN**
for background and alternate blocks

1-1/4 yards **MUSLIN** or coordinating
FLORAL PRINT for inner border (see Option*)

1-7/8 yards **GREEN PRINT** #2 for side
and corner triangles, and outer border

1/4 yard **GREEN FLORAL PRINT**
for corner squares

2/3 yard **GREEN PRINT** #2 for binding

5-1/4 yards **BACKING FABRIC**

Quilt batting, at least 64 x 92-inches

*Optional: Stencil from Stencil House,
Concord, NH (5-inch wide)
stencil paints, brush, and other supplies

*Note: Follow the fabric paint manufacturer's
instructions for stenciling on fabric or use coordinating
floral print fabric for the inner border strips.*

Basket Blocks

Make 7 **ROSE PRINT** Blocks
Make 8 **GREEN PRINT** #1 Blocks

*Note: As an option you could make all the basket
blocks a different color.*

Cutting
From ROSE PRINT:
- Cut 1, 6-7/8 x 42-inch strip.
- Cut 3, 2-7/8 x 42-inch strips.

From GREEN PRINT #1:
- Cut 1, 6-7/8 x 42-inch strip.
- Cut 3, 2-7/8 x 42-inch strips.

From MUSLIN:
- Cut 2, 6-7/8 x 42-inch strips.
- Cut 6, 2-7/8 x 42-inch strips.
- Cut 6, 2-1/2 x 42-inch strips.
  From these strips cut:
  30, 2-1/2 x 6-1/2-inch rectangles, and
  15, 2-1/2-inch squares.

Piecing

Step 1   With right sides together, layer the
6-7/8 x 42-inch **ROSE PRINT** strip
and a 6-7/8 x 42-inch **MUSLIN** strip.
Press together, but do not sew. Cut the
layered strip into squares. Cut the
layered squares in half diagonally

to make 8 sets of triangles (you will be using only 7 sets of triangles). Stitch 1/4-inch from the diagonal edge of the 7 pairs of triangles, and press. At this point each triangle-pieced square should measure 6-1/2-inches square.

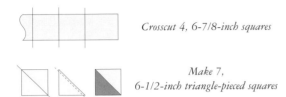

Crosscut 4, 6-7/8-inch squares

Make 7, 6-1/2-inch triangle-pieced squares

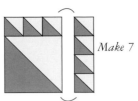

Make 7

Step 2 With right sides together, layer the 2-7/8 x 42-inch **ROSE PRINT** strips and 3 of the 2-7/8 x 42-inch **MUSLIN** strips in pairs. Press together, but do not sew. Cut the layered strips into squares. Cut the layered squares in half diagonally to make 63 sets of triangles. Stitch 1/4-inch from the diagonal edge of each pair of triangles, and press. At this point each triangle-pieced square should measure 2-1/2-inches square.

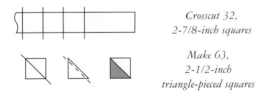

Crosscut 32, 2-7/8-inch squares

Make 63, 2-1/2-inch triangle-pieced squares

Step 3 Sew together 3 of the 2-1/2-inch triangle-pieced squares, and press. Referring to the Step 4 diagram, sew the units to the top edge of the 6-1/2-inch triangle-pieced squares, and press.

 *Make 7*

Step 4 Sew together 4 of the 2-1/2-inch triangle-pieced squares, and press. Sew the units to the right edge of the 6-1/2-inch triangle-pieced squares, and press.

Step 5 Referring to the block assembly diagram for placement, sew a 2-1/2-inch triangle-pieced square to a 2-1/2 x 6-1/2-inch **MUSLIN** rectangle. Sew this unit to the left edge of the basket unit, and press. Sew a 2-1/2-inch triangle-pieced square to the left edge of a 2-1/2 x 6-1/2-inch **MUSLIN** rectangle, and press. Add a 2-1/2-inch **MUSLIN** square to the left edge of the unit, and press. Sew this unit to the bottom of the basket unit to complete the basket block, and press. At this point each basket block should measure 10-1/2-inches square.

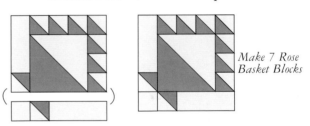

Make 7 Rose Basket Blocks

Step 6 In the same manner, make the **GREEN PRINT** #1 baskets. With right sides together, layer the 6-7/8 x 42-inch **GREEN PRINT** #1 strip and a 6-7/8 x 42-inch **MUSLIN** strip. Press together, but do not sew. Cut the layered strips into 4, 6-7/8-inch squares. Cut the layered squares in half diagonally to make 8 sets of triangles. Stitch 1/4-inch from the diagonal edge of each pair of triangles, and press. At this point each triangle-pieced square should measure 6-1/2-inches square.

Make 8, 6-1/2-inch triangle-pieced squares

Step 7 In the same manner, layer the 2-7/8 x 42-inch **GREEN PRINT** strips and 3 of the 2-7/8 x 42-inch **MUSLIN** strips in pairs. Press together, then cut the layered strips into 36, 2-7/8-inch squares. Cut the layered squares in half diagonally to make 72 sets of triangles. Stitch 1/4-inch from the diagonal edge of each pair of triangles, and press. At this point each triangle-pieced square should measure 2-1/2-inches square.

Make 72, 2-1/2-inch triangle-pieced squares

Step 8 Sew together 3 of the 2-1/2-inch triangle-pieced squares, and press. Referring to the block assembly diagram, sew the units to the top edge of the 6-1/2-inch triangle-pieced squares, and press.

Make 8

Step 9 Sew together 4 of the 2-1/2-inch triangle-pieced squares, and press. Referring to the block assembly diagram, sew the units to the right edge of the 6-1/2-inch triangle-pieced squares, and press.

Make 8

Step 10 Referring to the block assembly diagram for placement, sew a 2-1/2-inch triangle-pieced square to a 2-1/2 x 6-1/2-inch **MUSLIN** rectangle. Sew this unit to the left edge of the basket unit, and press. Sew a 2-1/2-inch triangle-pieced square to the left edge of a 2-1/2 x 6-1/2-inch **MUSLIN** rectangle, and press. Add a 2-1/2-inch **MUSLIN** square to the left

edge of the unit, and press. Sew this unit to the bottom of the basket unit to complete the basket block, and press. At this point each basket block should measure 10-1/2-inches square.

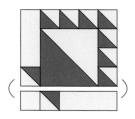 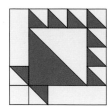

Make 8 Green Basket Blocks

Quilt Center

Note: The side and corner triangles are larger than necessary and will be trimmed before the borders are added.

Cutting

From **MUSLIN**:
- Cut 2, 10-1/2 x 42-inch strips.
  From these strips cut:
  8, 10-1/2-inch squares.

From **GREEN PRINT #2**:
- Cut 2, 17 x 42-inch strips.
  From these strips cut:
  3, 17-inch squares. Cut the squares diagonally into quarters for a total of 12 side triangles, and 2, 10-inch squares.
  Cut the squares in half diagonally for a total of 4 corner triangles.

Assembling the Quilt Center

Step 1 Referring to the quilt diagram, lay out the basket blocks, **MUSLIN** alternate blocks, and **GREEN PRINT #2** side triangles. Sew the pieces together in diagonal rows. Press the seam allowances away from the basket blocks.

Step 2 Pin the rows at the block intersections and sew the rows together. Press the seam allowances in one direction.

Step 3 Sew the **GREEN PRINT** #2 corner triangles to the quilt center, and press.

Step 4 Trim away the excess fabric from the side and corner triangles, taking care to allow a 1/4-inch seam allowance beyond the corners of each block. Refer to Trimming Side and Corner Triangles on page 200.

Borders

Note: The yardage given allows for the border strips to be cut on the crosswise grain. Diagonally piece the strips as needed, referring to page 203 for Diagonal Piecing Instructions.

Cutting

From **MUSLIN** or **FLORAL PRINT**:
• Cut 6, 6-1/2 x 42-inch inner border strips.

From **GREEN PRINT** #2:
• Cut 8, 3-1/2 x 42-inch outer border strips.

From **GREEN FLORAL PRINT**:
• Cut 4, 6-1/2-inch corner squares.

Stenciling and Attaching the Borders

Step 1 Measure the quilt center from left to right and cut 2, 6-1/2-inch wide **MUSLIN (or FLORAL PRINT)** strips to that length. If using **MUSLIN**, center the stencil on each strip and stencil. After the paint has dried, sew the stenciled border strips to the top and bottom edges of the quilt, and press.

Step 2 Measure the quilt center from top to bottom including the seam allowances but not the borders just added. Cut 2, 6 1/2 inch wide **MUSLIN (or FLORAL PRINT)** strips to that length. If using **MUSLIN**, center the stencil on each strip and stencil. After the paint has dried, add the 6-1/2-inch **GREEN FLORAL** corner squares to both ends of the stenciled border strips. Sew the stenciled border strips to the side edges of the quilt, and press.

Step 3 To attach the 3-1/2-inch wide **GREEN PRINT** #2 outer border strips, refer to page 202 for Border Instructions.

Putting It All Together

Cut the 5-1/4 yard length of **BACKING FABRIC** in half crosswise to form 2 lengths at least 2-5/8 yards long. Refer to Finishing the Quilt on page 203 for complete instructions.

Binding

From **GREEN PRINT** #2:
• Cut 8, 2-3/4 x 42-inch strips.

Sew the binding to the quilt using a 3/8-inch seam allowance. This measurement will produce a 1/2-inch wide finished double binding.

Refer to page 203 for Binding and Diagonal Piecing Instructions.

May Basket Quilt

For a spring spruce-up, even the garage can easily go from homely to homey. Lynette simply screened the garage window with a cost-effective 8-foot fence panel and used the balance of the wall for a potting table.

Spring
The leaves are
uncurling
My seedlings are
up. The sunlight
is warmer. Mine
got a new pup.
The robins are
building. I've painted
my bike. And we
can go barefoot
Whenever we like.

Kerry
Age 7

In a fitting tribute to spring, this child's Adirondack chair showcases a poem that Lynette's daughter Kerry penned at the age of seven. Lynette saved the original and much later had it stitched in embroidery and fabric-matted in a frame as a keepsake for Kerry.

Tulip Garden Quilt

FABRICS & SUPPLIES

Finished Size: 37-3/4 x 49-inches

Yardage is based on 42-inch wide fabric

5/8 yard **MUSLIN** for appliqué foundation

1-1/2 yards **BEIGE FLORAL**
for alternate blocks, side
and corner triangles, and outer border

1/4 yard **GREEN PRINT** for inner border

1/3 yard **SOLID GREEN**
for stem and leaf appliqués

3-inch squares of **36 ASSORTED PRINTS** for flower appliqués

1/2 yard **GREEN PRINT** for binding

1-1/2 yards **BACKING FABRIC**

Quilt batting, at least 42 x 53-inches

1/2 yard freezer paper for appliqué

Appliqué the Tulip Blocks

Make 6 Blocks

Note: Make a template of the entire flower shape to use as a Placement Guide for the individual flower shapes. To do so, photocopy the shape on page 63, glue the paper to a manila folder to stabilize it, and cut out the shape. Use the outer portion for the template and discard the inner portion.

Cutting

From **MUSLIN**:
- Cut 2, 8-3/4 x 42-inch strips.
  From these strips cut:
  6, 8-3/4-inch appliqué foundation squares.

From **SOLID GREEN**:
- Cut 6, 1-3/8 x 6-inch bias strips.
- Cut 6, 1-3/8 x 4-inch bias strips.

Appliqué the Stems

Step 1   Fold a 1-3/8 x 6-inch **SOLID GREEN** bias strip in half lengthwise with wrong sides together, and press. To keep the raw edges aligned, stitch 1/4-inch away from the edges. Fold the strip in half again so the raw edges are hidden by the first folded edge, and press. Position the Placement Guide on an 8-3/4-inch **MUSLIN** square, aligning bottom edges. Simply lay the stem inside this shape for placement. Pin the stem in place.

Step 2   In the same manner, prepare a 1-3/8 x 4-inch **SOLID GREEN** bias strip. Pin the stem in place on the **MUSLIN** square, tucking one end under the 6-inch long stem. Hand-stitch the stems in place. Make 6 blocks.

Flower and Leaf Appliqué
(Freezer Paper Technique)

Note: With this method of hand appliqué, the freezer paper forms a base around which each flower and leaf is shaped.

Step 1   Lay a piece of freezer paper, paper side up, over a leaf shape, and use a pencil to trace this shape 12 times. Cut out the leaves on the traced lines.

Step 2   With a dry iron on the wool setting, press the coated side of each freezer paper leaf onto the wrong side of the **SOLID GREEN** leaf fabric. Allow at least 1/2-inch between each shape for seam allowances.

Step 3   Cut out each leaf a scant 1/4-inch beyond the edge of the freezer paper pattern and finger-press the seam allowance over the edge of the freezer paper.

Step 4   Position 2 leaves on the **MUSLIN** square using the Placement Guide. Appliqué the leaves with matching thread. When there is about 3/4-inch left to appliqué on each leaf, slide your needle into this opening and loosen the freezer paper. Gently remove it, and finish stitching each leaf in place. Repeat on the remaining 5 **MUSLIN** squares.

Step 5   In the same manner, prepare the flower centers, trace 12 times. Appliqué the flower centers on the **MUSLIN** squares.

Step 6   In the same manner, prepare the flower petals, tracing 12 and 12 reversed. Appliqué the petals on the **MUSLIN** squares.

Quilt Center

Note: The side and corner triangles are larger than necessary and will be trimmed before the borders are added.

Cutting
From BEIGE FLORAL:
- Cut 1, 14 x 42-inch strip.
  From this strip cut:
  2, 14-inch squares. Cut the squares diagonally into quarters, forming 8 triangles. You will be using only 6 for side triangles.
- Cut 1, 9 x 42-inch strip.
  From this strip cut:
  2, 9-inch squares. Cut the squares in half diagonally for a total of 4 corner triangles, and
  2, 8-3/4-inch squares for the alternate blocks.

Assembling the Quilt Center

Step 1   Referring to the quilt diagram, sew together the 6 appliquéd blocks, 2 alternate blocks, and 6 side triangles in diagonal rows. Press the seam allowances in alternating directions by rows so the seams will fit snugly together with less bulk.

Step 2   Pin the rows at the block intersections, and sew the rows together. Press the seam allowances in one direction.

Step 3   Sew the 4 corner triangles to the quilt center, and press.

Step 4   Trim away the excess fabric from the side and corner triangles, taking care to allow a 1/4-inch seam allowance beyond the corners of each block. Refer to Trimming the Side and Corner Triangles on page 200 for complete instructions.

Borders

Note: The yardage given allows for the border strips to be cut on the crosswise grain. Diagonally piece the strips as needed, referring to page 203 for Diagonal Piecing Instructions.

Cutting

From GREEN PRINT:
- Cut 4, 1-1/2 x 42-inch inner border strips.

From BEIGE FLORAL:
- Cut 4, 6-1/2 x 42-inch outer border strips.

Attaching the Borders

Step 1   To attach the 1-1/2-inch wide **GREEN PRINT** inner border strips, refer to page 202 for Border Instructions.

Step 2   To attach the 6-1/2-inch wide **BEIGE FLORAL** outer border strips, refer to page 202 for Border Instructions.

Putting It All Together

Trim the backing and batting so they are 4-inches larger than the quilt top. Refer to Finishing the Quilt on page 203 for complete instructions.

Binding

Cutting

From GREEN PRINT:
- Cut 5, 2-3/4 x 42-inch strips.

Sew the binding to the quilt using a 3/8-inch seam allowance. This measurement will produce a 1/2-inch wide finished double binding.

Refer to page 203 for Binding and Diagonal Piecing Instructions.

Tulip Garden Quilt

Tulip Placement Guide

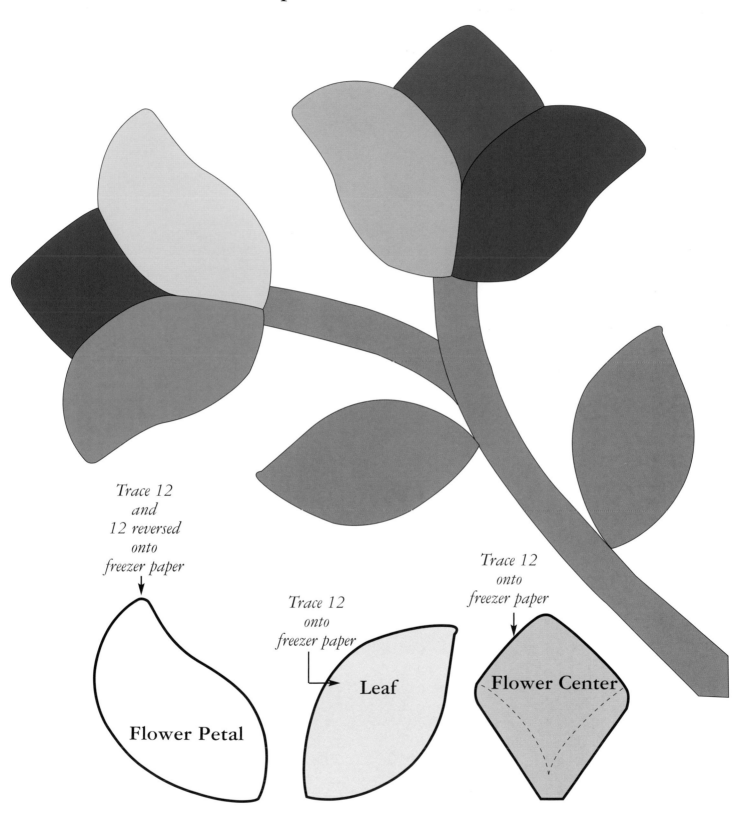

*Trace 12
and
12 reversed
onto
freezer paper*

Flower Petal

*Trace 12
onto
freezer paper*

Leaf

*Trace 12
onto
freezer paper*

Flower Center

Summer
Celebrations

"From the invitations to the decorations and food to the party favors, you'll find everything you need for a summer celebration."

For Lynette, living with classic country offers the opportunity to celebrate independence from rigid, traditional decorating rules, since almost anything goes.

With the emphasis on making family and guests feel comfortable and relaxed, Lynette makes a celebration seem almost effortless.

Lynette's guidelines are simple to follow. If your space is small, move everything to the great outdoors. If your space is large, bring everyone together in a cozy corner of the family room.

Regardless of the size of the room or the crowd, focus on making harmony the heart of the home.

On the pages that follow, Lynette takes you through the summer season with ideas and inspirations for informal old-fashioned fun celebrated in casual country-style. From the invitations, decorations, and food to the party favors, you'll find everything you need for a summer celebration.

Start your summer fun with a bridal shower for family or friends. The

romance of classic country style is in full bloom when it comes to hosting a bridal shower. Prior to her summer wedding, Lynette's daughter Kerry was the recipient of several bridal showers. Now as her friends anticipate marriage, she can reciprocate by helping them celebrate in a casual, but special way.

A gift box favor for each guest holds a photo frame for a photo-memory of the party to be sent to guests as a reminder of the festivities.

Turn the page for simple instructions and recipes for the bridal shower invitation, party favor gift boxes, and delicious desserts tempting enough to sweeten any summer celebration.

You Are Invited
to a
Bridal Shower!

Date
Saturday, June 16

Time

Even a simple invitation to a bridal shower becomes a keepsake with the addition of dried
flowers from the garden. For the invitation shown above, I collected mallow blossoms, pressed them between
the pages of a phone book, and glued them to the front of a folder created to hold the invitation.
If you are really "pressed for time," floral stickers can just as easily be substituted for the real thing.

SUPPLIES

Lidded Paper Maché Boxes

Cream Paint and Green Paint

Leaf Stencils and Brush

Gift Wrap Tissue

Purchased Photo Frame

Sheer Gold Ribbon

Dried Floral Blossoms

Gift Boxes

To make the gift boxes, Lynette and Kerry started with lidded paper maché boxes from the craft store. They painted each box cream and added a delicate border of stenciled leaves.

After a tissue-wrapped photo frame was nestled into each box, the lid was added and both box and lid tied together with an elegant sheer gold ribbon topped off with a nosegay of dried blossoms tucked into the bow.

Other suggestions for showering your guests with gifts include scented candles or potpourri, bath and body ensembles or your favorite chocolates.

Sugar Cookies

2 cups butter, softened

2 cups sugar

1 egg

1 tsp. vanilla

1/4 tsp. salt

1 tsp. baking powder

4-1/4 cups flour

Cream butter, sugar, egg and vanilla until fluffy. Combine dry ingredients; stir into creamed mixture just until blended. Divide and shape dough into four, 2-inch round logs. Refrigerate, covered, at least 2 hours or overnight.

Preheat oven to 375°. Slice roll into 1/4-inch slices and bake until edges are golden brown (approximately 8 minutes). Remove to wire rack to cool.

Makes 8–9 dozen.

Vanilla Creme Sauce

1 cup heavy whipping cream

1 cup sour cream

4 T. sugar

2 tsp. vanilla

Whisk to blend ingredients. Cover and refrigerate for several hours.

Tops 10–12 desserts.

Salted Nut Bars

1, 9 x 13-inch white cake

1, 8 oz. can honey roasted peanuts, chopped

Powdered Sugar Almond Frosting (from recipe below)

Cut cake into 18 pieces. Frost all sides with frosting. Place chopped nuts on waxed paper and roll frosted cake pieces in nuts, coating all sides. Allow frosting to dry slightly before serving.

Makes 18.

Powdered Sugar Almond Frosting

2 cups powdered sugar

1/3 cup milk

1 tsp. almond extract

Mix until smooth. Use to frost salted nut bars or your favorite cakes and cookies.

Table Settings

Easy but elegant. Sometimes setting a festive table requires only the extra touch of a rolled linen napkin, ribbon-tied and accented with a tiny dried rosebud.

(Note: working with a small piece of the same kind of ribbon used for the party favor gift box will give a coordinated look to each place setting.)

Decorating for summer celebrations is surprisingly simple with soft comforts that lend an air of nostalgia to any room.

Lynette brings a bit of summer sunshine to every nook and cranny with little decorating ideas for big impact.

Union Square Quilt

Union Square Blocks

Make 25 Blocks

Cutting

From each of the 25 **ASSORTED MEDIUM PRINTS**:

- Cut 1, 4-1/2 x 42-inch strip.
  From this strip cut:
  1, 4-1/2-inch square,
  4, 2-1/2 x 4-1/2-inch rectangles, and
  2, 2-7/8-inch squares.
- Cut 1, 2-1/2 x 42-inch strip.
  From this strip cut:
  16, 2-1/2-inch squares.

From **MUSLIN**:

- Cut 35, 2-1/2 x 42-inch strips.
  From these strips cut:
  200, 2-1/2 x 4-1/2-inch rectangle, ands
  200, 2-1/2-inch squares.
- Cut 4, 2-7/8-inch x 42-inch strips.
  From these strips cut: 50, 2-7/8-inch squares

Piecing

For each Union Square block you will need eight 2-1/2 x 4-1/2-inch **MUSLIN** rectangles, eight 2-1/2-inch **MUSLIN** squares, four 2-1/2-inch triangle-pieced squares, and one set of **MEDIUM PRINT** pieces (one 4-1/2-inch square, four 2-1/2 x 4-1/2-inch rectangles, and sixteen 2-1/2-inch squares).

Step 1   Position a 2-1/2-inch **MEDIUM PRINT** square on the corner of a 2-1/2 x 4-1/2-inch **MUSLIN** rectangle. Draw a diagonal line on the **MEDIUM PRINT** square, and stitch on the line. Trim the seam allowance to 1/4-inch, and press. Repeat this process at the opposite corner of the **MUSLIN** rectangle. Make 8 units. Sew the units

FABRICS & SUPPLIES

Finished Size: 85-inches square

Yardage is based on 42-inch wide fabric

5-3/4 yards **MUSLIN** for blocks, side triangles, corner triangles, middle border, and outer border

1/3 yard each of 25 **ASSORTED MEDIUM PRINTS** for blocks

7/8 yard **GREEN PRINT** for narrow borders

3/4 yard **MUSLIN** for binding

7-1/2 yards **BACKING FABRIC**

Quilt batting, at least 89-inches square

Optional: Purchased embroidery patterns to transfer onto the muslin side triangles and embroidery floss.

together in pairs, and press. At this point each unit should measure 4-1/2-inches square.

Make 8   *Make 4*

Step 2   Position a 2-1/2-inch **MUSLIN** square on the left-hand corner of a 2-1/2 x 4-1/2-inch **MEDIUM PRINT** rectangle. Draw a diagonal line on the **MUSLIN** square, and stitch on the line. Trim the seam allowance to 1/4-inch, and press.

     Make 4

Step 3   With right sides together, layer a 2-7/8-inch **MEDIUM PRINT** square and a 2-7/8-inch **MUSLIN** square. Press together, but do not sew. Cut the layered square in half diagonally to make 2 sets of triangles. Stitch 1/4-inch from the diagonal edge of the 2 pairs of triangles, and press. Repeat this process with the remaining 2-7/8-inch **MEDIUM PRINT** and **MUSLIN** squares. Sew a 2-1/2-inch **MUSLIN** square to the left edge of each triangle-pieced square, and press. At this point each unit should measure 2-1/2 x 4-1/2-inches.

Make 4, 2-1/2-inch triangle-pieced squares   *Make 4*

Step 4   Sew a Step 3 unit to the top of a Step 2 unit, and press. Make 4 units. At this point each unit should measure 4-1/2-inches square.

Make 4

Step 5   Referring to the block diagram, sew a Step 1 unit to both sides of the 4-1/2-inch **MEDIUM PRINT** square, and press. Sew a Step 4 unit to both sides of the remaining Step 1 units, and press. Sew the 3 horizontal rows together to make a block. At this point the block should measure 12-1/2-inches square.

Step 6   Repeat Steps 1 through 5 to make a total of 25 Union Square blocks.

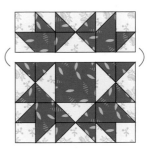

Quilt Center

Note: The side and corner triangles are larger than necessary and will be trimmed before the borders are added.

Cutting

From MUSLIN:

- Cut 2, 19 x 42-inch strips. From these strips cut: 3, 19-inch squares. Cut the squares diagonally into quarters for a total of 12 side triangles, and 2, 10-inch squares. Cut the squares in half diagonally for a total of 4 corner triangles.

Assembling the Quilt Center

Step 1   Referring to the quilt diagram, lay out the Union Square blocks and **MUSLIN** side triangles. Sew the pieces together in diagonal rows. Press the seam allowances in alternating directions by rows so the seams will fit snugly together with less bulk.

Step 2 Pin the rows at the block intersections and sew the rows together. Press the seam allowances in one direction.

Step 3 Sew the **MUSLIN** corner triangles to the quilt center, and press.

Step 4 Trim away the excess fabric from the side and corner triangles, taking care to allow a 1/4-inch seam allowance beyond the corners of each block. Refer to Trimming the Side and Corner Triangles on page 200.

Borders

Note: The yardage given allows for the border strips to be cut on the crosswise grain. Diagonally piece the strips as needed, referring to page 203 for Diagonal Piecing Instructions.

Cutting

From GREEN PRINT:

- Cut 16, 1-1/2 x 42-inch narrow border strips.

From MUSLIN:

- Cut 8, 1-1/2 x 42-inch middle border strips.
- Cut 9, 6 x 42-inch outer border strips.

Attaching the Borders

Step 1 To attach the first 1-1/2-inch wide **GREEN PRINT** narrow border strips, refer to page 202 for Border Instructions.

Step 2 To attach the 1-1/2-inch wide **MUSLIN** middle border strips, refer to page 202 for Border Instructions.

Step 3 To attach the second 1-1/2-inch wide **GREEN PRINT** narrow border strips, refer to page 202 for Border Instructions.

Step 4 To attach the 6-inch wide **MUSLIN** outer border strips, refer to page 202 for Border Instructions.

Putting It All Together

Cut the 7-1/2 yard length of **BACKING FABRIC** into thirds crosswise to form 3, 2-1/2 yard lengths.

Refer to Finishing the Quilt on page 203 for complete instructions.

Binding

Cutting

From MUSLIN:

- Cut 9, 2-3/4 x 42-inch strips.

Sew the binding to the quilt using a 3/8-inch seam allowance. This measurement will produce a 1/2-inch wide finished double binding.

Refer to page 203 for Binding and Diagonal Piecing Instructions.

Union Square Quilt

vintage embroidery and crochet
Basket Pillow

When Lynette discovered the yellow crocheted basket that her grandmother had started but never finished, she quickly turned it into a project. The clever combination of crochet and pieced embroidery scraps resulted in a one-of-a-kind keepsake pillow for her daughter Kerry's home.

Pillow Front

To make the pillow front, Lynette sewed together a variety of embroidered pieces and then trimmed the piece to 18-1/2-inches square. She hand-tacked a crocheted basket to this pieced square to complete the pillow front.

Pillow Ruffle

Cutting

From **BLUE PRINT**:
• Cut 5, 3 x 42-inch strips.

Attaching the Ruffle

Step 1   Diagonally piece the 3-inch wide **BLUE PRINT** strips together to make a continuous ruffle strip, referring to page 203 for Diagonal Piecing Instructions.

Step 2   Fold the strip in half lengthwise, wrong sides together, and press. Divide the ruffle strip into 4 equal segments, and mark the quarter points with safety pins.

Step 3   To gather the ruffle, position a heavy-weight thread (or 2 strands of regular weight sewing thread) 1/4-inch in from the raw edges of the folded ruffle.

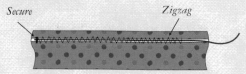

Secure   *Zigzag*

Note: You will need a length of heavyweight thread 144-inches long. Secure one end of the thread by stitching across it. Zigzag-stitch over the thread all the way around the ruffle, taking care not to sew through it.

Step 4   With right sides together, pin the ruffle to the pillow front, matching the quarter points of the ruffle to the corners of the pillow front. Pull up the gathering stitches until the ruffle fits the pillow front, taking care to allow fullness in the ruffle at each corner. Sew the ruffle to the pillow front, using a scant 1/4-inch seam allowance.

Pillow Back

Cutting

From **BLUE PRINT**:
• Cut 2, 18-1/2 x 22-inch rectangles.

Assembling the Pillow Back

Step 1   With wrong sides together, fold the 2, 18-1/2 x 22-inch **BLUE PRINT** rectangles in half to form 2, 11 x 18-1/2-inch double-thick pillow back pieces. Overlap the 2 folded edges by about 4-inches so the pillow back measures 18-1/2-inches square, and pin. Stitch around the entire piece to create a single pillow back, using a scant 1/4-inch seam allowance.

Step 2   With right sides together, layer the pillow back and the pillow front, and pin. The ruffle will be turned toward the center of the pillow at this time. Stitch around the outside edges using a 3/8-inch seam allowance.

Step 3   Trim the pillow back and corner seam allowances if needed. Turn the pillow right side out and fluff up the ruffle. Insert the pillow form through the back opening.

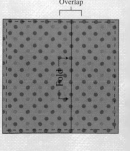

Overlap

Fold

Several years ago Lynette and Neil Jensen welcomed a once-in-a-lifetime opportunity to purchase their two-story Colonial nestled in a neighborhood filled with historic houses. The house offered Lynette the opportunity to restore another old house and establish numerous flower gardens.

As an added incentive, the house was majestically situated on a hill overlooking the bend of a river. The backyard has become a cherished hideaway offering a commanding view of the Crow River which meanders gently through their small town. While affording privacy, the tree-lined retreat is also sized right for large gatherings of friends and family for special summer celebrations.

Coordinating a Collection

Before recovering your furniture or investing in new upholstered pieces, Lynette suggests an easy way to see if a coordinating collection of stripes, prints, plaids, and solids really work well together. Simply combine the fabrics randomly on the fronts and backs of pillows for the patio. Stitch up a stack of oversized pillows to mix and match— you'll soon discover your favorite combination.

For the tabletop
centerpiece, Lynette
parks plants on an old
shutter and the slant
of the slats easily
allows for drainage and
proper air circulation.

At sunset, small pails
painted and stenciled
are home to citronella
candles which ward
off pesky mosquitoes
while providing a
romantic glow for
celebrating long
summer evenings.

"Indoors or out, creating a special summer place for parties on the porch often requires more imagination than money."

Lynette believes that indoors or out, creating a special summer place for parties on the porch often requires more imagination than money.

She leads the way in this porch filled with an eclectic mix of old and older, all costing much less than if purchased new. For instance, Lynette counts the table in the foreground as one of the best garage-sale buys to date.

A friend who is also an experienced garage-sale shopper found this table and at first glance it was so beat up that even she failed to take notice. However, on thinking it over she decided

to go back the next day and see if this diamond- in- the- rough was still available for the magnificent sum of 25 cents. To her delight, remaining items from the sale had been marked down to half price. She took the table home for 12-1/2 cents!

Lynette now counts it as one of the all-time favorite gifts she has received.

Lynette experimented

with coats of paint and a sailboat stencil inspired by glasses passed down from her grandmother Halverson for a fresh yet heritage finish.

Other oldies but goodies include the tin lunch pails, wicker picnic baskets, and toy tops and drum.

Sailboat Table

Paint table with a light color such as beige latex paint. Paint table with a second coat of medium-blue latex paint.

Let dry overnight and sand lightly with medium-grain sand paper to reveal some of the lighter color underneath. On edges that would show wear on a vintage piece, sand off some of both coats revealing raw wood.

Stencil boat and star design as desired.

With a rag, apply a coat of medium stain and wipe off excess immediately. The stain will give the table finish a little patina and will settle the stencil into the surface.

Allow to dry completely. To protect from wear and moisture apply a coat of matte finish polyurethane.

Lamp Shade Trim

Measure circumference of lamp shade both at the top and bottom. Add 2-inches to each measurement.

Cut 2 bias strips 1-1/2-inches wide by the length of above measurements.

Press each strip in half lengthwise creasing slightly.

Unfold and press each lengthwise raw edge to center fold.

Apply white fabric glue to bottom edge of lamp shade applying a narrow line of glue around the shade edge.

Align fabric binding on right side of shade with center fold on edge of shade.

To finish and cover raw edge of binding end, fold under end of bias strip and overlap raw end of bias strip. Extra glue needs to be applied at this point to secure.

Apply another line of glue on the inside edge of the shade and fold bias strip to inside of shade pressing firmly to glued edge.

Repeat for top edge trim of the lamp shade.

The best way to celebrate summer that Lynette can imagine is a porch filled with things made by hand—from the crocheted rug on the floor to the Midnight Sky quilt complete with shining stars.

Lynette loves to buy an inexpensive lamp and then give it personality by stenciling summer flowers on the base and adding a country-plaid binding to the shade.

Oval Crocheted Rug

FABRICS & SUPPLIES

Finished Size: 43 x 53-inches

Yardage is based on 42-inch wide fabric

25 yards of ASSORTED FABRICS

Crochet hook size N

These instructions have been verbally passed on for years from generation to generation—Since all fabrics vary as does the tension of each person's stitches, it is necessary to increase as needed to prevent the rug from cupping.

The ultimate goal is to have a nice flat rug without waves or ripples. Practice definitely makes each rug better than the first!

Preparing the Fabric Strips

Step 1   Cut the fabric into 1-1/4 x 42-inch strips.

Step 2   Sew the strips together securely end to end.

Step 3   Fold the strips in half lengthwise, wrong sides together, and roll into several balls, each about 4 inches in diameter.

Crocheting the Rug

Step 1   Loosely ch 18 sts

Step 2   To turn, sc 2 sts in 2nd ch from last st

Step 3   Loosely sc in each ch st along strip up to the last st

Step 4   In last ch st, loosely sc 3 sts

Step 5   Loosely sc along other side of chain

Step 6   In last ch st, sc 2 st, in the next 2 sts, sc 2 st (6 sts)

Step 7   Continue sc, increase at the ends as needed. Repeat the same increase at the opposite end. Never increase at the sides.

Step 8   When the rug is desired size, hide the loose strip ends in the backside of the rug. Use a smaller crochet hook to work the strips into the stitches.

Making and Attaching the Fringe

Step 1   Cut 1-1/4 x 11-inch strips from the assorted fabrics.

Step 2   Fold each strip in half lengthwise and then in half crosswise. Using the crochet hook, pull the folded end through one-outer stitch of the rug. Slip the free ends of the strip through the loop that was formed and pull to tighten. Repeat for each outer stitch.

One of Lynette's favorite hobbies is crocheting oval rag rugs using fabric scraps from quilting projects to make rag balls. The rag balls shown here have been passed on to Lynette from the supply her grandmother kept on hand.

Lynette learned to sew strips of fabric together for rag balls on her grandmother's treadle sewing machine.

Cutting

From the **RED PRINT**:
- Cut 1, 20-1/2 x 36-1/2-inch rectangle for inner pillowcase.

From the **RED PLAID**:
- Cut 1, 20-1/2 x 36-1/2-inch rectangle for outer pillowcase.
- Cut 4, 3 x 18-1/2-inch strips for ties.

Assemble the Inner Pillowcase

Step 1 To make the hem on the **RED PRINT** fabric, turn one long edge under 1 inch, and press. Turn the same edge under 1 inch again and press. Topstitch in place to finish the pillow case hem.

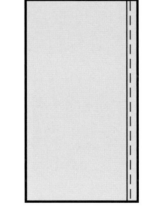

Step 2 With right sides together, fold the hemmed rectangle in half and sew the raw edges together using a 1/4-inch seam allowance. Turn the pillowcase right side out. Insert the pillow form, and hand-stitch the opening closed.

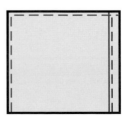

Fold

FABRICS & SUPPLIES

Finished Size: 18-inches square
Yardage is based on 42-inch wide fabric

2/3 yard **RED PRINT** fabric
for inner pillowcase

1 yard **RED PLAID**
fabric for outer pillowcase

18-inch square pillow form

Assemble the Outer Pillowcase

Step 1 Hem the 20-1/2 x 36-1/2-inch **RED PLAID** rectangle in the same manner as for the inner pillowcase.

Step 2 Repeat Step 2 as for the inner pillowcase, but do not insert the pillow form or hand-stitch the opening closed.

Step 3 To make each of the ties, fold one short end of 3 x 18-1/2-inch **RED PLAID** strip under 1/4-inch, and press. Fold the long edges under to meet at the center.

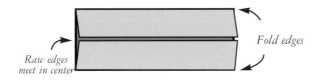

Raw edges meet in center — *Fold edges*

Step 4 Fold the strip in half lengthwise again, and stitch 1/8-inch away from the folded edges. At this point the tie should measure 3/4 x 18-1/2-inches.

Folded edges

Step 5 Insert the raw edges of the ties 1-1/4-inch to the inside of each side of the opening of the outer pillowcase, taking care to space them evenly. Stitch the ties in place along the edges of the pillowcase and through the hem.

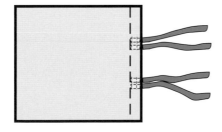

Step 6 Insert the inner pillow into the outer pillowcase, and tie each of the ties in a bow.

Picnic baskets, bird houses, and Fourth of July flags are sure signs of summer, and what retreat would be complete without a few of these old favorites?

For the porch, Lynette aptly demonstrates how festive red, white, and green can transcend the seasons for a rousing salute to summer!

Spark culinary fireworks with summertime favorites. Make it your best Fourth of July ever with flags, food, and fun before the evening fireworks. Gather friends and family following the community celebration for a sumptuous buffet. Garden-fresh vegetables are used as table decor, and an old childhood wagon holding plants and flowers adds to the spirit of fun. The picnic table, a hand-me-down from Lynette's mother, which has been white-washed and stenciled with stars and rays, says it all—Celebrate!

Above, the vintage blue enameled pail fits nicely into the same-style pan. Both are filled with shaved ice to hold chilled beverages.

Below, a vintage blue kettle is large enough to hold a mixture of garden flowers and herbs for an explosion of parade day color.

fun, food, and family
Parade Day Picnic

When it comes to summer celebrations, I'm the first to say, "Hurray for the red, white, and blue."
A quilted runner and flag napkins set the secene for the patriotic fun and food to come. These
projects work up quickly, especially the napkins featuring a small parade flag in the center block.

Picnic Table Runner

Make 3 Blocks

Cutting

From GOLD PRINT:

- Cut 1, 4-1/2 x 42-inch strip.
  From this strip cut:
  3, 4-1/2-inch squares.
- Cut 3, 2-1/2 x 42-inch strips.
  From these strips cut:
  36, 2-1/2-inch squares.

From BLUE GRID:

- Cut 1, 2-1/2 x 42-inch strip.
  From this strip cut:
  12, 2-1/2-inch squares.
- Cut 2, 2-1/2 x 42-inch strips.
  From these strips cut:
  12, 2-1/2 x 4-1/2-inch rectangles.

From RED PRINT:

- Cut 3, 2-1/2 x 42-inch strips.

From BEIGE PRINT:

- Cut 2, 1-1/2 x 42-inch strips.

Piecing

Step 1   Position a 2-1/2-inch **GOLD PRINT** square on the corner of a 2-1/2 x 4-1/2-inch **BLUE GRID** rectangle. Draw a diagonal line on the **GOLD PRINT** square, and stitch on the line. Trim the seam allowance to 1/4-inch, and press. Repeat this process at the opposite corner of the **BLUE GRID** rectangle.

Make 12 star points

Step 2   Sew Step 1 star point units to the top and bottom of a 4-1/2-inch **GOLD PRINT** square. Press the seam allowances toward the **GOLD PRINT** square. Sew 2-1/2-inch **BLUE GRID** squares to the ends of the remaining star point units. Press the seam allowances toward the **BLUE GRID** squares. Sew the units to the sides of the star unit, and press.

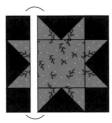

Make 3

Step 3   Aligning long edges, sew together the 2-1/2 x 42-inch **RED PRINT** strips and 1-1/2 x 42-inch **BEIGE PRINT** strips. Press the seam allowances toward the **RED PRINT** strips. Cut the strip set into segments.

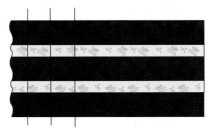

Crosscut 12, 2-1/2-inch wide segments

Step 4   Sew Step 3 units to the top and bottom of the star units, and press. Add 2-1/2-inch **GOLD PRINT** squares to the ends of the remaining Step 3 units, and press. Sew the units to the sides of the star units to complete each star block, and press.

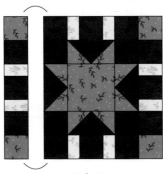

Make 3

Quilt Center and Border

Note: The yardage given allows for the border strips to be cut on the crosswise grain. Diagonally piece the strips as needed, referring to page 203 for Diagonal Piecing Instructions.

Cutting

From **BLUE PRINT**:
- Cut 4, 5-1/2 x 42-inch border strips.
- Cut 1, 2-1/2 x 42-inch strip.
  From this strip cut:
  2, 2-1/2 x 12-1/2-inch lattice strips.

Assembly

Step 1   Sew together the 3 pieced blocks and the 2-1/2 x 12-1/2-inch **BLUE PRINT** lattice strips, and press.

Step 2   To attach the 5-1/2-inch wide **BLUE PRINT** border strips, refer to page 202 for Border Instructions.

Putting It All Together

Trim the **BACKING FABRIC** and batting so they are 4-inches larger than the runner top. Refer to Finishing the Quilt on page 203 for complete instructions.

Binding

Cutting

From **RED PRINT**:
- Cut 4, 2-3/4 x 42-inch strips.

Sew the binding to the quilt using a 3/8-inch seam allowance. This measurement will produce a 1/2-inch wide finished double binding. Refer to page 203 for Binding and Diagonal Piecing Instructions.

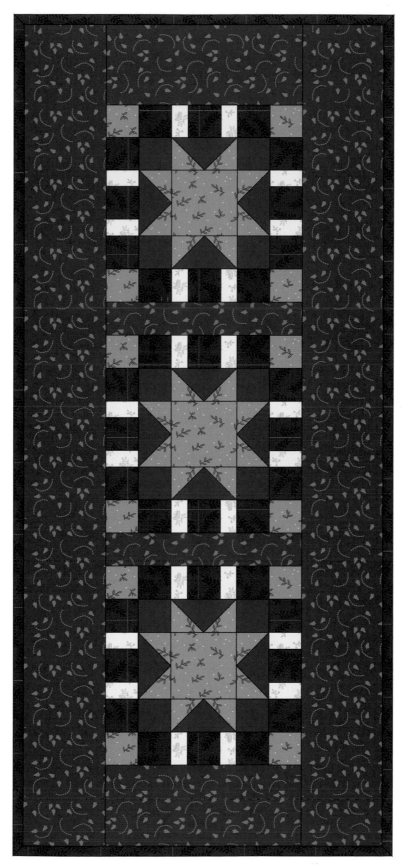

Picnic Table Runner

Flag Napkins

Piecing

Step 1 Sew 4-1/2-inch wide **GOLD PRINT** borders to the top and bottom of the flag, and press. Trim the ends even with the flag.

Step 2 Sew 3-inch wide **GOLD PRINT** borders to the sides of the flag, and press. Trim the ends even with the flag. Repeat for a total of 4 napkin fronts.

Make 4

Step 3 With right sides together, layer a 16-1/2-inch pieced napkin front and a 16-1/2-inch **BLUE PRINT** square napkin back. Sew 1/4-inch from the cut edges, leaving 3-inches open on one side for turning.

Step 4 Clip the corners, turn the napkin right side out and press, taking care to see that the corners are sharp and even. Hand-stitch the opening closed.

Step 5 Stitch diagonally from corner to corner to stabilize the napkin.

Step 6 Repeat Steps 3 through 5 to make a total of 4 napkins.

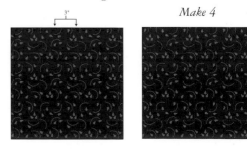

Make 4

FABRICS & SUPPLIES

Finished Size: 16-inches square

Yardage is based on 42-inch wide fabric

7/8 yard **GOLD PRINT** for border

1 yard **BLUE PRINT** for napkin back

4, 8-1/2 x 11-1/2-inch flags

Note: Alter the fabric measurements if using a different size flag.

Makes 4 Napkins

Cutting

From **GOLD PRINT**:
- Cut 3, 4-1/2 x 42-inch border strips.
- Cut 4, 3 x 42-inch border strips.

From **BLUE PRINT**:
- Cut 2, 16-1/2 x 42-inch strips.
  From these strips cut: 4, 16-1/2-inch squares.

Pecan Biscotti

2-1/2 cups flour

1-1/2 tsp. baking powder

1/2 tsp. salt

1 tsp. ground cinnamon

1/2 cup unsalted butter at room temperature

1 cup sugar

3 eggs

1 T. vanilla

1/2 tsp. almond extract

2 cups toasted pecans, coarsely chopped

Preheat oven to 325°. Stir together the flour, baking powder, salt and cinnamon. Set aside. In another bowl, combine butter and sugar using an electric mixer. Beat until light and fluffy. Add eggs one at a time, beating well after each one. Beat in vanilla and almond extracts.

Stir in the flour mixture, beating in one-third at a time at low speed. Fold in nuts.

Divide dough in half and place on a floured work surface. Roll each half into an oval log about 1-1/2-inches in diameter and 12-inches long. Place 1/2-inch apart on an ungreased baking sheet.

Bake about 30 minutes or until golden brown. Remove from oven and let cool until comfortable to touch.

Reduce oven temperature to 250°.

Cut each log on the diagonal into slices 1-inch thick. Place slices, cut side down on the ungreased baking sheet and return to oven. Bake until lightly toasted and the edges are golden brown (about 10 minutes). Let cool.

Can be made 3 to 5 days in advance of serving and stored in an airtight container. If they do soften, recrisp by placing them in a 250° oven.

Makes 20–24 pieces.

Chicken or Turkey Salad

1, 7 oz. pkg. macaroni rings or shells

3 cups cooked chicken or turkey, cubed

1 cup grated carrots

1 cup diced celery

1 medium onion, diced

1/2 cup each: sliced radishes, diced green pepper, green olives, and parsley

Dressing:

1-1/2 cups mayonnaise

1/4 cup lemon juice

1/3 cup sugar

1 tsp. salt

Dash of pepper

Cook macaroni according to package instructions. Mix dressing ingredients; pour over the macaroni, chicken and vegetables; mix well.

Makes 8 servings.

Harvest Homecoming

"The change of seasons is welcome because it means bringing in the outdoors with gatherings from my garden."

Autumn has always been Lynette's favorite season of the year. Even before the first twirling leaf drifts to the ground, she has been busy transforming her house and garden into a veritable cornucopia of seasonal scent, color, texture, and sentiment. Discover how Lynette's ideas for using simple materials—from candles and collectibles to pictures and pillows—will inspire you. Celebrate this season of plenty with a feast of colorful autumn accents in your home and garden.

September ushers in autumn with the crisp scent of cool mornings that warm to sunny afternoons—just right for gathering nature's abundant harvest.

To create a special welcome, wheel in fall foliage by the bushels. Oversize planters, such as this copper washtub, accommodate an abundance of hardy fall plantings that will bloom late into the season. Petite pumpkins are golden accents for nearly every harvest arrangement.

Inside her garden house, Lynette manages to arrange her busy schedule around a constant parade of fall flowers drying on racks and in containers of many shapes and sizes. She freely combines abundant quantities of drieds from October's golden harvest to make casual autumn arrangements—the greater the variety of colors and textures the better.

On the pages that follow, see how easily you can create your own harvest homecoming inspired by decorating details from Lynette's favorite season of the year—autumn.

Pumpkin Presentation

Display gourd-pumpkin jack-o-lanterns on a trellis of Morning Glory vine and leaves. Here, an iron plant cage serves as a basket for pumpkins and gourds. It is the perfect height for elevating the vibrant orange of the pumpkins to mix with evergreens and fall flowers.

Tuck pumpkins
in among flowering
plants and evergreens—
bringing fall color to
parts of the garden
that ordinarily no longer
have colorful blooms.

Several years ago
Lynette discovered white
pumpkins and asked a
local farmer to grow
them for her.
They have since
become quite popular
and add nice contrast
to the landscape.

Pumpkins, real and imagined (on Lynette's Harvest Time quilt), abound in displays throughout the house at harvest time. Lynette selects pumpkins of all shapes and sizes and then chooses a palette of warm country colors ranging from toasty browns to deep shades of goldenrod.

Early in October, a wizard's hat serves as a pleasant reminder that tricks and treats are just around the corner. Adirondack chairs provide plenty of parking space for displays.

Lynette's palette of warm country colors ranging from toasty browns to deep shades of goldenrod are just as effective in her collection of pottery as in her fabric choices. Another accent that brings the harvest theme indoors is the framed wool appliqué pumpkin project.

Create the tiny tabletop display using a lidless black cookie jar topped by a Jack Frost pumpkin which casts an erie shadow by candlelight on the wall.

an autumn accent
Wool Pumpkin Picture

Feel free to mix and match. Simply combine a medley of sizes, shapes, and colors that work together to create charming country-style harvest themes. A variety of collected treasures is unified by color—the simplest design principle of all.

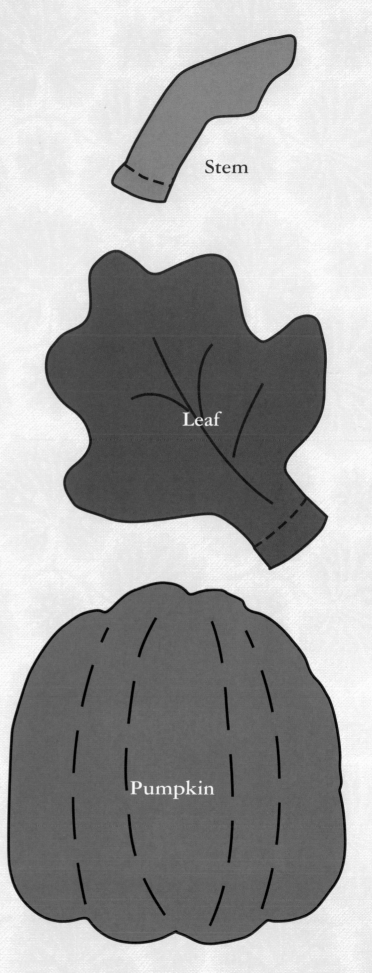

FABRICS & SUPPLIES

Yardage is based on 42-inch wide fabric

Piece of **WOOL** to fit frame for background

Scraps of **ASSORTED WOOLS** for appliqués

#8 tan and black

Perle cotton or embroidery floss
for decorative stitches

Template material

Appliqué the Pumpkin Picture

Step 1   Trace the appliqué shapes onto the
template material and cut out. Using
the templates, trace each shape onto the
WOOL fabrics, and cut out.

Step 2   Position the **WOOL** shapes on the wool
background piece, and appliqué in place
with the buttonhole stitch and black
perle cotton or 3 strands of embroidery
floss. Stem-stitch the leaf veins with black
perle cotton or 3 strands of embroidery
floss. Stem-stitch the tendrils with tan
perle cotton or 3 strands of embroidery
floss. Straight stitch the pumpkin sections
with black perle cotton or 3 strands of
embroidery floss. The decorative stitch
diagrams can be found on page 202.

Step 3   We suggest that you take your appliquéd
pumpkin picture and frame to a good frame
shop to have them do the assembly. The
piece shown is not covered with glass.

Paired with an antique wooden bowl, freshly painted papier-maché pumpkins are crackle-finished to look old. Lynette enjoys the challenge of finding ways to quickly transform an entire room such as the kitchen with seasonal accents in a matter of minutes.

Prime examples of her quick-change artistry are kitchen towels accented with sunflower and pumpkin motifs. By using light and dark shades of fabrics, Lynette creates the illusion of several different pumpkins from one simple pattern.

Appliquéd Tea Towels

Fusible Web Appliqué

Step 1   Trace the appliqué shapes on the paper
side of the fusible web, leaving 1/2-inch
between each shape. Cut the shapes
apart, leaving a small margin beyond
the drawn lines.

Step 2   Following the manufacturer's
instructions, apply the fusible web

shapes to the wrong side of the fabrics
chosen for the appliqués. Let the
fabrics cool and cut on the traced line.
Peel away the paper backing from the
fusible web.

Step 3   Referring to the photograph, position
the appliqué shapes on the tea towel,
and fuse in place.

Step 4   The tea towels shown were machine-
appliquéd using matching thread and a
zigzag stitch.

Optional: Buttonhole stitch around the shapes
using perle cotton or 3 strands of embroidery
floss. The Decorative Stitch diagram is found on
page 202.

*Note: To prevent the buttonhole stitches from "rolling
off" the edges of the appliqué shapes, take an
extra backstitch in the same place as you make
the buttonhole stitch, going around outer
curves, corners, and points. For straight edges,
taking a backstitch every inch is enough.*

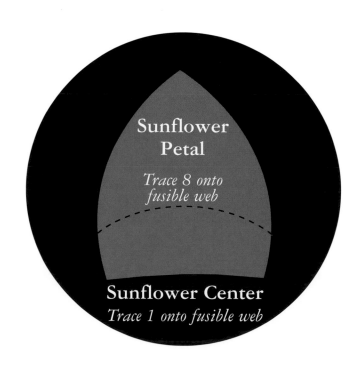

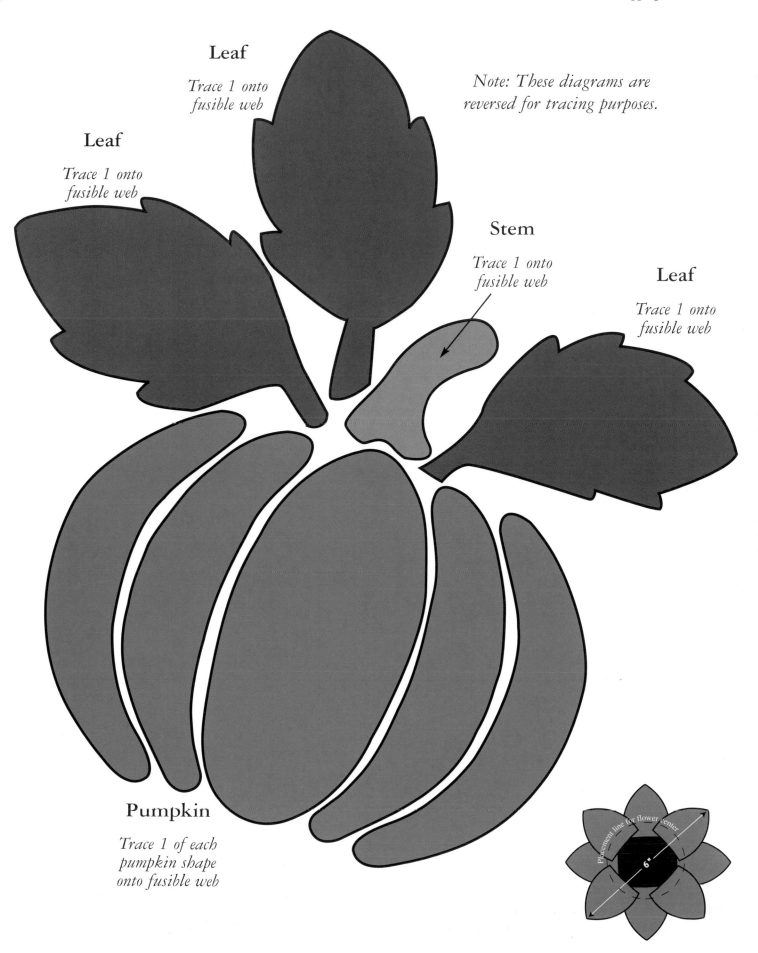

Leaf

Trace 1 onto fusible web

Leaf

Trace 1 onto fusible web

Note: These diagrams are reversed for tracing purposes.

Stem

Trace 1 onto fusible web

Leaf

Trace 1 onto fusible web

Pumpkin

Trace 1 of each pumpkin shape onto fusible web

Placement line for flower center

6"

Framing a small quilt, such as the Pumpkins for Sale wallhanging quilt shown above, creates a seasonal backdrop. The collectibles gracing the dining room sideboard draw colors from the fabrics—tying it all together for a festive display.

Leaf A

(Make 3)

Cutting

From GREEN PRINT #1, ONE CHESTNUT PRINT, and ONE RED PRINT:
- Cut 1, 1-1/2 x 3-1/2-inch rectangle each.
- Cut 1, 1-1/2 x 2-1/2-inch rectangle each.
- Cut 2, 1-1/2-inch squares each.
- Cut 1, 3/4 x 2-1/2-inch strip each.

From BEIGE PRINT:
- Cut 3, 1-3/4-inch squares. Cut the squares in half diagonally for a total of 6 triangles.
- Cut 3, 1-1/2 x 2-1/2-inch rectangles.
- Cut 9, 1-1/2-inch squares.

Piecing

Step 1 Position a 1-1/2-inch **GREEN PRINT #1** square on the corner of a 1-1/2 x 2-1/2-inch **BEIGE PRINT** rectangle. Draw a diagonal line on the **GREEN PRINT #1** square, and stitch on the line. Trim the seam allowance to 1/4-inch, and press. Repeat this process at the opposite corner of the **BEIGE PRINT** rectangle. Sew a 1-1/2-inch **BEIGE PRINT** square to the right-hand side of this unit, and press.

Step 2 Position a 1-1/2-inch **BEIGE PRINT** square on the corner of the 1-1/2 x 3-1/2-inch **GREEN PRINT #1** rectangle. Draw a diagonal line on the square and stitch on the line. Trim the seam allowance to 1/4-inch, and press.

Step 3 Position a 1-1/2-inch **BEIGE PRINT** square on the corner of the 1-1/2 x 2-1/2-inch **GREEN PRINT #1** rectangle. Draw a diagonal line on the square and stitch on the line. Trim the seam allowance to 1/4-inch, and press.

Step 4 To make the **GREEN PRINT #1** stem unit, center a 1-3/4-inch **BEIGE PRINT** triangle on the 3/4 x 2-1/2-inch **GREEN PRINT #1** strip. Stitch a 1/4-inch seam, trim and press. Repeat on the other side of the **GREEN PRINT #1** strip. Press the seam allowances toward the stem. Trim the ends of the **GREEN PRINT #1** stem. At this point the stem unit should measure 1-1/2-inch square. Sew the Step 3 unit to the right-hand side of the stem unit, and press.

Step 5　Referring to the block diagram, sew together the units from Step 1, 2, and 4, and press. At this point Leaf A should measure 3-1/2-inches square.

Step 6　For the **CHESTNUT PRINT** and **RED PRINT** Leaf A blocks, repeat Steps 1 through 5.

Leaf B

(Make 4)

Cutting

From 2 **GREEN PRINTS**, one **CHESTNUT PRINT**, and one **RED PRINT**:

- Cut 1, 1-7/8-inch square each.
- Cut 1, 1-1/2 x 3-1/2-inch rectangle each.
- Cut 1, 1-1/2 x 2-1/2-inch rectangle each.
- Cut 1, 1-1/2-inch square each.
- Cut 1, 3/4 x 2-1/2-inch strip each.

From **BEIGE PRINT**:

- Cut 4, 1-7/8-inch squares.
- Cut 4, 1-3/4-inch squares. Cut the squares in half diagonally for a total of 8 triangles.
- Cut 8, 1-1/2-inch squares.

Piecing

Step 1　Layer together a 1-7/8-inch **BEIGE PRINT** and a **GREEN PRINT** square. Cut the layered square in half diagonally. Stitch 1/4-inch from the diagonal edge of each pair of triangles, and press. Sew the triangle-pieced squares together, then add a 1-1/2-inch **GREEN PRINT** square to the right-hand side of this unit, and press.

Make 2, 1-1/2-inch triangle-pieced squares

Step 2　Position a 1-1/2-inch **BEIGE PRINT** square on the corner of a 1-1/2 x 3-1/2-inch **GREEN PRINT** rectangle. Draw a diagonal line on the square; stitch on the line. Trim the seam allowance to 1/4-inch; press.

Step 3　Position a 1-1/2-inch **BEIGE PRINT** square on the corner of a 1-1/2 x 2-1/2-inch **GREEN PRINT** rectangle. Draw a diagonal line on the square and stitch on the line. Trim the seam allowance to 1/4-inch and press.

Step 4　To make the **GREEN PRINT** stem unit, refer to Leaf A, Step 4. Sew the Step 3 unit to the right-hand side of the stem unit, and press.

Step 5　Referring to the block diagram, sew together the units from Step 1, 2, and 4, and press. At this point Leaf B should measure 3-1/2-inches square.

Step 6　For the remaining **GREEN PRINT**, **CHESTNUT PRINT**, and **RED PRINT** Leaf B blocks, repeat Steps 1 through 5.

Pumpkins

Cutting

From **ORANGE PRINT #1**:

- Cut 1, 4-1/2 x 5-1/2-inch rectangle.

From **ORANGE PRINT #2**:

- Cut 1, 2-3/8 x 2-7/8-inch rectangle.
- Cut 1, 2-1/2 x 7-1/2-inch rectangle.
- Cut 1, 2-1/2-inch square.
- Cut 1, 1-1/2 x 6-1/2-inch rectangle.
- Cut 3, 1-1/2-inch squares.

From **BEIGE PRINT**:

- Cut 1, 2-7/8-inch square.
- Cut 1, 2-1/2-inch square.
- Cut 5, 1-1/2-inch squares.

From **GREEN PRINT #1**:
- Cut 1, 1-1/2 x 2-1/2-inch rectangle.
- Cut 1, 1-1/2-inch square.
- Cut 1, 1 x 2-7/8-inch rectangle.
- Cut 1, 1-inch square.

Piecing

Step 1   Position 3, 1-1/2-inch **ORANGE PRINT #2** squares and 1, 1-1/2-inch **BEIGE PRINT** square on the corners of the 4-1/2 x 5-1/2-inch **ORANGE PRINT #1** rectangle, as shown. Draw a diagonal line on the squares and stitch on these lines. Trim the seam allowances to 1/4-inch, and press.

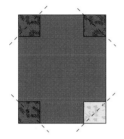 

Step 2   Position 2, 1-1/2-inch **BEIGE PRINT** squares on the corners of the 1-1/2 x 6-1/2-inch **ORANGE PRINT #2** rectangle, as shown. Draw diagonal lines on the squares and stitch on these lines. Trim the seam allowances to 1/4-inch, and press. Set this unit aside to be used in the Quilt Center section.

Step 3   Position a 1-1/2-inch **BEIGE PRINT** square on the corner of the 2-1/2 x 7-1/2-inch **ORANGE PRINT #2** rectangle. Draw a diagonal line on the **BEIGE PRINT** square and stitch on the line. Trim the seam allowance to 1/4-inch, and press.

Step 4   Position a 1-1/2-inch **GREEN PRINT #1** square on the corner of the 2-1/2-inch **ORANGE PRINT #2** square. Draw a diagonal line on the **GREEN PRINT #1** square and stitch on the line. Trim the seam allowance to 1/4-inch, and press. Repeat at the opposite corner of the **ORANGE PRINT #2** square with the 1-inch **GREEN PRINT #1** square, as shown.

Make 1

Step 5   Sew the 1 x 2-7/8-inch **GREEN PRINT #1** rectangle to the left-hand side of the 2-3/8 x 2-7/8-inch **ORANGE PRINT #2** rectangle, and press. Layer the 2-7/8-inch **BEIGE PRINT** square on this unit. Cut the layered square in half diagonally. Stitch a 1/4-inch seam along the diagonal edge of the lower triangle, as shown, and press. Sew this unit to the right-hand side of the Step 4 unit, and press.

Make 1

Make 1

Step 6   Position a 1-1/2-inch **BEIGE PRINT** square on the corner of the 1-1/2 x 2-1/2-inch **GREEN PRINT #1** rectangle. Draw a diagonal line on the **BEIGE PRINT** square and stitch on the line. Trim the seam allowance to 1/4-inch, and press. Sew this unit to the right-hand side of the 2-1/2-inch **BEIGE PRINT** square as shown, and press.

Make 1

Quilt Center

Cutting

From **BEIGE PRINT**:
- Cut 4, 2-1/2 x 3-1/2-inch rectangles.
- Cut 1, 1-1/2 x 3-1/2-inch rectangle.

Quilt Center Assembly

Referring to the quilt assembly diagram, lay out the leaf blocks, pumpkin sections, and **BEIGE PRINT** rectangles. For the left-hand section, sew the pieces together in horizontal rows, and press. Sew the rows together, and press. For the right-hand section, sew the pieces together in vertical rows, and press. Sew the sections together, and press. At this point the quilt center should measure 12-1/2-inches square.

Borders

Note: The yardage given allows for the border strips to be cut on the crosswise grain. Diagonally piece the strips as needed, referring to page 203 for Diagonal Piecing Instructions.

Cutting

From **BROWN PRINT #1**:
- Cut 2, 1-1/2 x 42-inch strips for the inner border.

From **BROWN PRINT #2**:
- Cut 2, 1-7/8 x 42-inch strips for the sawtooth border.
- Cut 3, 1 x 42-inch strips for the narrow middle border.

From **BEIGE PRINT**:
- Cut 2, 1-7/8 x 42-inch strips for the sawtooth border.
- Cut 4, 1-1/2-inch squares for the sawtooth corner squares.

From **GREEN PRINT #2**:
- Cut 5, 2-1/2 x 42-inch strips for the wide middle border and outer border.

Attaching the Borders

Step 1 To attach the 1-1/2-inch wide **BROWN PRINT #1** inner border strips, refer to page 202 for Border Instructions.

Step 2 To make the sawtooth border, layer the 1-7/8 x 42-inch **BROWN PRINT #2** and **BEIGE PRINT** strips together in pairs. Press them together, but do not sew. Cut the layered strips into squares.

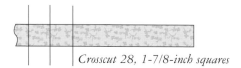

Crosscut 28, 1-7/8-inch squares

Step 3 Cut the layered squares in half diagonally. Stitch 1/4-inch from the diagonal edge of each pair of triangles, and press. At this point each triangle-pieced square should measure 1-1/2-inches square.

Make 56, 1-1/2-inch triangle-pieced squares

Step 4 Sew 14 triangle-pieced squares together for each sawtooth border strip, and press. Sew 2 of the borders to the top and bottom of the quilt, and press.

Step 5   Add 1-1/2-inch **BEIGE PRINT** squares to both ends of the remaining sawtooth borders, and press. Sew these borders to the sides of the quilt, and press.

Step 6   To attach the 2-1/2-inch wide **GREEN PRINT** #2 middle border strips, refer to page 202 for Border Instructions.

Step 7   To attach the 1-inch wide **BROWN PRINT** #2 narrow middle border strips, refer to page 202 for Border Instructions.

Step 8   To attach the 2-1/2-inch wide **GREEN PRINT** #2 outer border strips, refer to page 202 for Border Instructions.

Putting It All Together

Trim the **BACKING FABRIC** and batting so they are about 2-inches larger than the quilt top. Refer to Finishing the Quilt on page 203 for complete instructions.

Binding

Cutting

From **ORANGE PRINT#1**:
- Cut 3, 2-3/4 x 42-inch strips.

Sew the binding to the quilt using a 3/8-inch seam allowance. This measurement will produce a 1/2-inch wide finished double binding. Refer to page 203 for Binding and Diagonal Piecing Instructions.

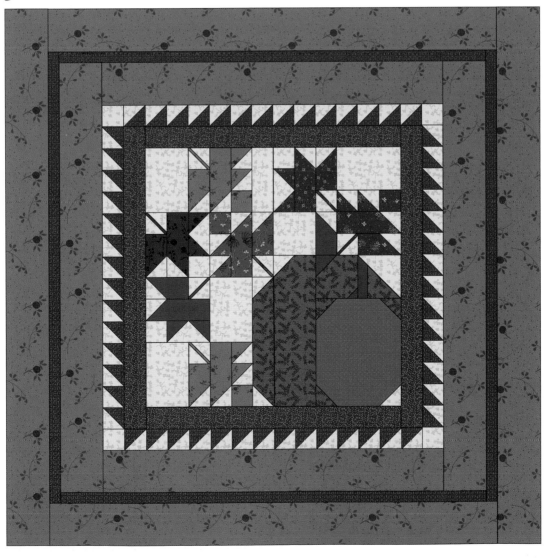

Pumpkins for Sale

Drying Flowers

Over the years Lynette has found that the easiest way to dry most flowers is to pick them when they are at their peak. Hang them upside down in a dry location away from direct sunlight.

For hydrangeas, pick them in late summer, just as they dry on the plant. When they feel like parchment paper they are ready to cut.

Every autumn, Lynette anticipates a full harvest of her own homegrown hydrangeas to add color, texture, and volume to dried floral arrangements.

Lynette's Harvest Pinwheels quilt is the perfect color complement to an antique plant stand brimming with dried blooms.

Harvest Blocks

Make 12 Blocks

Cutting

From **BROWN PRINT**:
- Cut 9, 2-7/8 x 42-inch strips.

From **BEIGE PRINT #1**:
- Cut 9, 2-7/8 x 42-inch strips.

From **GREEN PRINT #1**:
- Cut 6, 2-1/2 x 42-inch strips.
  From these strips cut:
  48, 2-1/2 x 4-1/2-inch rectangles.

From **GOLD PRINT**:
- Cut 6, 2-1/2 x 42-inch strips.
  From these strips cut:
  96, 2-1/2-inch squares.

Piecing

Step 1   Layer together the 2-7/8 x 42-inch **BROWN PRINT** and **BEIGE PRINT** strips in pairs. Press together; do not sew. Cut the layered strips into squares.

Crosscut 120, 2-7/8-inch layered squares

Step 2   Cut the layered squares in half diagonally. Stitch 1/4-inch from the diagonal edge of each pair of triangles, and press. At this point each triangle-pieced square should measure 2-1/2-inches square.

Make 240, 2-1/2-inch triangle-pieced squares

Step 3   Referring to the diagram, sew triangle-pieced squares together in pairs, and press. Make 24 pairs. Sew the pairs

FABRICS & SUPPLIES

Finished Size: 63-inches square

Yardage is based on 42-inch wide fabric

1 yard **BROWN PRINT**
for pinwheels and sawtooth

1 yard **BEIGE PRINT** #1 for block background

1/2 yard **GREEN PRINT** #1 for blocks

3/4 yard **GOLD PRINT**
for blocks and first inner border

5/8 yard **BEIGE PRINT** #2 for center square

3/4 yard **RED PRINT** for second inner border, lattice, and narrow outer border

1-1/2 yards **GREEN PRINT** #2
for third inner border and wide outer border

2/3 yard **RED PRINT** for binding

4 yards **BACKING FABRIC**

67-inch square quilt batting

together and press to complete the pinwheel unit. At this point the pinwheel unit should measure 4-1/2-inches square.

Make 12

Step 4 Sew 2-1/2 x 4-1/2-inch **GREEN PRINT #1** rectangles to the top and bottom of the pinwheel unit, and press. Add 2-1/2-inch **GOLD PRINT** squares to both ends of the remaining 2-1/2 x 4-1/2-inch **GREEN PRINT #1** rectangles, and press. Sew these units to the sides of the block, and press. At this point the block should measure 8-1/2-inches square.

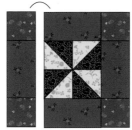

Make 12

Step 5 Sew 4, Step 2 triangle-pieced squares together for each sawtooth border, and press.

Make 48

Step 6 Sew a sawtooth border to the top and bottom of the block, and press. Add a 2-1/2-inch **GOLD PRINT** square to both ends of the remaining sawtooth borders, and press. Sew a sawtooth border to both sides of the block, and press. At this point the block should measure 12-1/2-inches square.

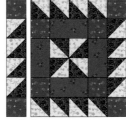

Make 12

Inner Borders

Note: The yardage given allows for the border strips to be cut on the crosswise grain. Diagonally piece the strips as needed, referring to page 203 for Diagonal Piecing Instructions.

Cutting

From **BEIGE PRINT #2**:
• Cut 1, 17-1/2-inch center square.

From **GOLD PRINT**:
• Cut 2, 2-1/2 x 42-inch strips for first inner border.

From **RED PRINT**:
• Cut 3, 1-1/2 x 42-inch strips for second inner border.

From **GREEN PRINT #2**:
• Cut 4, 2-1/2 x 42-inch strips for third inner border.

Attaching the Inner Border Strips

Step 1 To attach the 2-1/2-inch wide **GOLD PRINT** inner border strips to the quilt, refer to page 202 for Border Instructions.

Step 2 To attach the 1-1/2-inch wide **RED PRINT** inner border strips to the quilt, refer to page 202 for Border Instructions.

Step 3 To attach the 2-1/2-inch wide **GREEN PRINT #2** inner border strips to the quilt, refer to page 202 for Border Instructions.

Quilt Center

Cutting

From **RED PRINT**:
• Cut 4, 1-1/2 x 42-inch strips. From these strips cut: 12, 1-1/2 x 12-1/2-inch lattice strips.

Assemble the Quilt Center

Step 1 Sew together 2 blocks and 3, 1-1/2 x 12-1/2-inch **RED PRINT** lattice strips, and press. Make 2 block rows, and sew them to the top and bottom of the quilt center, and press.

Step 2 Sew together 4 blocks and 3, 1-1/2 x 12-1/2-inch **RED PRINT** lattice strips, and press. Make 2 block rows and sew them to the sides of the quilt center, and press.

Outer Borders

Note: The yardage given allows for the border strips to be cut on the crosswise grain. Diagonally piece the strips as needed, referring to page 203 for Diagonal Piecing Instructions.

Cutting

From **RED PRINT**:

- Cut 6, 1-1/2 x 42-inch narrow outer border strips.

From **GREEN PRINT#2**:

- Cut 7, 5-1/2 x 42-inch wide outer border strips.

Attaching the Borders

Step 1 To attach the 1-1/2-inch wide **RED PRINT** narrow outer border strips to the quilt, refer to page 202 for Border Instructions.

Step 2 To attach the 5-1/2-inch wide **GREEN PRINT #2** wide outer border strips to the quilt, refer to page 202 for Border Instructions.

Putting It All Together

Cut the 4 yard length of **BACKING FABRIC** in half crosswise to make 2, 2 yard lengths. Refer to Finishing the Quilt on page 203 for complete instructions.

Binding

Cutting

From **RED PRINT**:

- Cut 7, 2-3/4 x 42-inch strips.

Sew the binding to the quilt using a 3/8-inch seam allowance. This measurement will produce a 1/2-inch wide finished double binding. Refer to page 203 for Binding and Diagonal Piecing Instructions.

Harvest Pinwheels Quilt

Vintage Halloween
decorations are back
by popular demand.
For display dimension,
showcase them on a
shelf filled with an
assortment of whimsical
orange and black accents
and candy-filled crockery
bowls to match.

Turn your home

into Halloween

headquarters with

the many faces

of the season!

Not just for kids, Halloween is a time to invite friends and family to a pumpkin carving party followed by a Sunday Night Supper (see page 138). Include both events on an invitation printed on heavy paper, cut out using a novelty paper edger, and mounted on black corrugated paper. Insert the invitation into a fabric bag that can later be used for holding treats.

Reviving childhood memories, Kerry and Trevor discover that pumpkin carving can still be a lot of fun even for hardworking young professionals. Here the newspaper topped picnic table comes indoors and a Log Cabin Quilt adds warmth to the walls.

no trick to this treat
Popcorn Balls

At Halloween, let the fun times begin with popcorn balls sweetened with candy corn accents. For an easy,
no-bake treat, toss in a handful of cookie ghosts—packaged oval peanut butter cookies dipped in melted white chocolate.
For custom serving, arrange vintage papers under the glass of an antique wooden tray painted black.

Popcorn Balls

2 cups white sugar

1 cup corn syrup

1/2 tsp. cream
of tartar

1 T. butter

1/2 tsp. baking soda

6 quarts popped corn

Combine and cook first 4 ingredients to hardball stage using a candy thermometer. Remove from heat and add baking soda. Pour over popped corn and toss to coat.

When cool enough to touch but still warm, butter hands and form balls approximately 3-inches in diameter. When cool, wrap in cellophane and store in airtight container.

Makes 18–24 popcorn balls.

For late-autumn accents that add interest and warmth to your front yard or patio, put the focus on white pumpkins. Then add to the mix an old copper tub filled with water, floating leaves, and candles cleverly disguised as miniature pumpkins and apples.

For an interesting companion accent, paint an old wooden chair a deep, warm red color and set the chair and copper tub outdoors near your home's entrance.

You'll find this recipe for apple crisp the perfect complement to your harvest-time meals.

Apple Crisp

6 apples, peeled and sliced

3/4 cup sugar

1 tsp. cinnamon

1/3 cup melted butter

1 cup flour

1 cup brown sugar

Mix apples, sugar and cinnamon. Place in a greased deep dish pie plate. Combine butter, flour, and brown sugar. Pat over top of apples. Bake 45 minutes at 350 °. Top with whipped cream or ice cream.

Serves 8.

family friendly and crowd pleasing
Tasty Treats

Keeping sandwich fixings and the cookie jar filled with homemade cookies is a constant challenge for Lynette when son, Matt, comes home to visit (and snack!). My mother gave us the old green jar when Neil and I moved into our first house. Over the years I've tried to first fill the house with love, and then fill the cookie jar with fresh-baked favorites from our families' recipes—such as the Ginger Snaps cookies Matt is more than happy to taste-test for me."

Ginger Snaps

3/4 cup shortening

1 cup sugar

1/4 cup light molasses

1 egg

2 cups flour

2 tsp. baking soda

1 tsp. cinnamon

1 tsp. cloves

1 tsp. ginger

1/4 tsp. salt

Cream shortening and sugar. Add egg and molasses, beat well. Stir dry ingredients together and mix well. Shape into 1-1/2-inch balls, dip in sugar. Place 2-inches apart on ungreased baking sheet. Bake 10–12 minutes at 350°.

Makes 48 cookies.

Raisin Cookies

1 cup sugar

1 cup shortening

1 cup raisins

5 tsp. raisin juice

2 eggs

1-1/2 cups oatmeal

1-1/2 cups flour

1 tsp. soda

1 tsp. cinnamon

1 tsp. cloves

chopped walnuts (optional)

Add 1 cup boiling water to raisins to soften and plump up. Let stand while creaming sugar and shortening.

Drain water off, reserving 5 tsp. raisin juice. Add raisins, juice, eggs and oatmeal to sugar and shortening.

Blend soda, cloves, and cinnamon with the flour and add to mixture. Stir in chopped walnuts. Drop by rounded teaspoons onto greased cookie sheet.

Bake for 8 to 11 minutes at 375 °.

Makes 48 cookies.

Focaccia Sandwich

1 loaf Focaccia bread

8 oz. sliced ham

8 oz. sliced smoked turkey

4 oz. hard salami

2 T. olive oil

1 onion, sliced

1 tomato, sliced

1 lb. provalone cheese

Slice bread in half, horizontally. Sauté onion in olive oil and place on bottom half of bread. Layer remaining ingredients, ending with cheese and tomatoes. Place top half of bread on layered meats, cheese and tomato.

Wrap in foil and bake at 325 ° for 20 to 30 minutes.

Cut loaf into 8 wedges. Serve warm.

Makes 8 servings.

Harvest suppers celebrating the gathering in of newly-harvested crops haven't changed much over the years. Main recipe ingredients are hearty autumn favorites such as the harvest popcorn, wild rice soup, and caramel apple cake shown here. Creating a clever place card holder to coordinate with the pumpkin patchwork napkin is as simple as placing a miniature pumpkin in a candy corn-filled ramekin. Copper wire, curled by wrapping it around a wooden spoon handle, holds the card.

Wild Rice Soup

2 med. stalks celery, sliced

1 med. carrot, coarsely shredded

1 med. onion, chopped (about 1/2 cup)

1 small green pepper, chopped

2 T. margarine or butter

3 T. all-purpose flour

1 tsp. salt

1/4 tsp. pepper

1-1/2 cups cooked wild rice

2 cups chicken broth

1 cup whole cream

1/3 cup toasted slivered almonds

1/4 cup snipped parsley

4 slices thick, lean bacon, cooked and crumbled

Cook wild rice following package directions. Cook and stir celery, carrot, onion and green pepper in margarine in 3-quart saucepan until celery is tender (about 5 minutes). Stir in flour, salt and pepper. Add chicken broth slowly, stirring constantly to blend in flour. Add wild rice. Heat to boiling.

Cover and simmer, stirring occasionally, 15 minutes. Stir in cream, almonds, parsley and bacon. Heat just until hot, but do not boil.

Makes 5 servings, about 1 cup each.

Note: May add cooked, diced chicken for a heartier soup.

Harvest Popcorn

4 quarts popped corn

1, 9 oz. can shoestring potatoes

2 T. melted butter

1/2 tsp. garlic powder

1/2 tsp. dried dill

Mix popcorn and shoestring potatoes in large mixing bowl.

Combine butter, garlic powder and dill. Pour mixture over popcorn and toss to coat evenly.

Makes 6 servings.

Caramel Apple Cake

1-1/2 cups vegetable oil

3 eggs

2 cups sugar

2 tsp. vanilla

3 cups flour

1 tsp. soda

1 tsp. salt

1-1/2 cups chopped pecans

3 cups peeled, diced apples

Combine oil, eggs, sugar and vanilla. Mix until well blended. Combine flour, soda and salt and add to egg mixture. Beat with mixer until completely blended. Fold in apples and pecans. The batter will be quite stiff. Spoon batter into a well greased and floured bundt pan.

Bake at 350° for 1 hour and 20 minutes. Leave cake in pan until completely cool, then invert onto cake plate. Top with caramel topping.

Makes 12–16 servings.

Caramel Topping

1/2 cup packed brown sugar

1/4 cup milk

1/2 cup butter

Mix and bring to a slow rolling boil. Cook for 3 minutes. Let sauce rest for 5 minutes. Drizzle over cake.

Salted Peanut Cookies

1 cup brown sugar

1 cup white sugar

1 cup shortening

2 eggs

1-1/2 tsp. vanilla

1 tsp. baking powder

1 tsp. baking soda

2 cups flour

1 cup corn flakes, well crushed

1 cup quick cooking oatmeal

1 cup salted Spanish peanuts

Cream together brown and white sugars with shortening. Beat eggs, and add to creamed mixture along with the vanilla.

Sift together flour, baking powder and soda and combine with creamed mixture. Stir in corn flakes, oatmeal, and peanuts. Roll into balls. Place on cookie sheet and flatten slightly.

Bake at 375° for about 12 minutes.

Makes 48 cookies.

One thing that remains

constant in the formal living

room are the black- and -cream

buffalo check upholstered chairs

and couch. Because they provide

the perfect backdrop for a variety

of seasonal decorating accents,

Lynette never tires of them.

For the several weeks leading

up to Thanksgiving Day,

the living room furniture in this

inviting setting is host to

quilts in deep shades of rust and

brown, accented with pillows

featuring pumpkin and leaf motifs.

When guests gather for dinner, greet them with a welcoming sight—personalized place cards nestled in gifts-to-go containers.

Amber is nature's gold. Create an elegant harvest table by accenting cream and sage with glistening amber.

Warm wood tones used in the framed collectibles unify this harvest grouping, which includes an antique turkey print. Showcase dishes with striking motifs to use as seasonal accents. The cupboard, below, holds an inviting display including transferware in a bold turkey pattern.

For each season, establish family traditions with favorite dishes, foods, and accessories.

Holiday Housewarming

"For me, Christmas is a time for sharing meaningful holiday traditions with family and friends."

During the Christmas holidays, Lynette Jensen transforms her home into a magical winter wonderland filled with the spirit of the season—love, joy, and peace.

Lynette's real countdown to Christmas begins just after Thanksgiving day, but she plans far ahead for holiday preparations that allow her plenty of time to enjoy the festivities with family and friends.

With careful planning and an emphasis placed on simplicity by using "what you already have on hand," Lynette's decorating, entertaining, and quilting inspirations for celebrating Christmas all through the house are a delight to one and all. As Lynette shares them with you, discover for yourself how easy it is to experience the true joys of Christmas!

As you look forward to this very special season, on the following pages discover how Lynette fills room after room with meaningful holiday traditions that blend whites with brights for festive, unified decorating upstairs, downstairs, and from the front porch to the back porch. Lynette's desire is that from the moment guests first arrive, they are treated to Christmas joy outside and inside her home.

Weeks before the first guests arrive, however, the living room has been transformed into a fairyland of lights and decorations. Soft accents like quilts and stockings are in traditional red and green, contrasting nicely with the black-and-cream upholstery.

an easy holiday accent
December Tree Pillow

In the living room, I always display a framed German die-cut Christmas greeting on the wall by the fireplace.
The fabrics in the quilt and pillow were chosen to coordinate with it. For a fast decorating accent or Christmas gift,
the rotary-cut and strip-pieced "December Tree" block on the pillow top works up quickly, even for beginners.

FABRICS & SUPPLIES

Finished Size: 16-inches square

Yardage is based on 42-inch wide fabric

1/4 yard **BEIGE PRINT** for background

1/4 yard **GREEN PRINT** for tree

3/8 yard **RED PRINT** for tree base
and inner ruffle

5/8 yard **TAN PRINT** for border
and pillow back

3/8 yard **GREEN PLAID** for outer ruffle

1/2 yard **MUSLIN** for backing of pillow top

Quilt batting, at least 18-inches square

16-inch pillow form

A rotary cutter, mat, and wide
clear plastic ruler with 1/8-inch markings

Pillow Top

Cutting

From **BEIGE PRINT**:
- Cut 2, 4-1/2 x 6-1/2-inch rectangles.
- Cut 2, 4-1/2-inch squares.
- Cut 2, 2-1/2-inch squares.
- Cut 2, 2-1/2 x 4-1/2-inch rectangles.

From **GREEN PRINT**:
- Cut 1, 4-1/2 x 8-1/2-inch rectangle.
- Cut 1, 4-1/2 x 12-1/2-inch rectangle.
- Cut 1, 2-1/2 x 12-1/2-inch rectangle.

From **RED PRINT**:
- Cut 1, 2-1/2 x 8-1/2-inch rectangle.

From **TAN PRINT**:
- Cut 2, 2-1/2 x 42-inch strips.
  From these strips cut:
  2, 2-1/2 x 12-1/2-inch border strips, and
  2, 2-1/2 x 16-1/2-inch border strips.

Piecing

Step 1   Position a 4-1/2 x 6-1/2-inch **BEIGE PRINT** rectangle on the left-hand corner of the 4-1/2 x 8-1/2-inch **GREEN PRINT** rectangle. Draw a diagonal line on the **BEIGE PRINT** rectangle, and sew on the line. Trim the seam allowance to 1/4-inch, and press. Repeat this process on the right-hand corner of the GREEN Print rectangle.

Make 1

Step 2   Position the 4-1/2-inch **BEIGE PRINT** squares on the corners of the 4-1/2 x 12-1/2-inch **GREEN PRINT** rectangle. Draw a diagonal line on the **BEIGE PRINT** squares, and stitch on the line. Trim the seam allowance to 1/4-inch, and press.

Make 1

153

Step 3   Position the 2-1/2-inch **BEIGE PRINT** squares on the corners of the 2-1/2 x 12-1/2-inch **GREEN PRINT** rectangle. Draw a diagonal line on the **BEIGE PRINT** squares, and stitch on the line. Trim the seam allowance to 1/4-inch, and press.

Make 1

Step 4   Position the 2-1/2 x 4-1/2-inch **BEIGE PRINT** rectangles on the corners of the 2-1/2 x 8-1/2-inch **RED PRINT** rectangle. Draw a diagonal line on the **BEIGE PRINT** rectangles, and stitch on the line. Trim the seam allowance to 1/4-inch, and press.

Make 1

Step 5   Sew together the Step 1 through 4 units, and press. At this point the tree block should measure 12-1/2-inches square.

Step 6   Sew a 2-1/2 x 12-1/2-inch **TAN PRINT** border strip to the top and bottom of the tree block, and press. Sew a 2-1/2 x 16-1/2-inch **TAN PRINT** border strip to the sides of the tree block, and press.

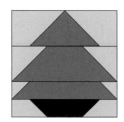

Putting It All Together

Step 1   Trim the **MUSLIN** backing and batting so they are 2-inches larger than the pillow top dimensions.

Step 2   Layer the **MUSLIN** backing, batting, and pillow top. Baste the layers together and quilt as desired.

Step 3   When quilting is complete, trim the excess backing and batting even with the pillow top.

Note: To prepare the pillow top before attaching the ruffle, Lynette suggests hand basting the edges of all 3 layers of the pillow top together. This will prevent the edge of the pillow top from rippling when you attach the ruffle.

Pillow Ruffle

Note: By sewing 2 different width fabrics together, you form the illusion of a double ruffle without all the additional bulk.

Cutting
From **RED PRINT**:
• Cut 4, 2-1/2 x 42-inch inner ruffle strips.

From **GREEN PLAID**:
• Cut enough 3-inch wide bias strips to measure 170-inches long for the outer ruffle strips.

Piecing and Attaching the Ruffle

Step 1   Diagonally piece together the 2-1/2-inch wide **RED PRINT** strips.

Step 2   Diagonally piece together the 3-inch wide **GREEN PLAID** strips.

Step 3   Sew the **RED PRINT** and **GREEN PLAID** strips together along a long edge, and press.

Step 4   With right sides facing, sew the short raw edges together with a diagonal seam to make a continuous ruffle strip.

Trim the seam allowance to 1/4-inch, and press.

Step 5 Fold the strip in half lengthwise, wrong sides together, and press. Divide the ruffle strip into 4 equal segments, and mark the quarter points with safety pins.

Step 6 To gather the ruffle, position a heavy-weight thread (or 2 strands of regular weight sewing thread) 1/4-inch from the raw edge of the folded ruffle strip.

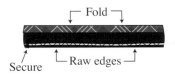

Note: *You will need a length of thread 2 times the circumference of the pillow. Secure one end of the heavy thread by stitching across it. Then zigzag stitch over the thread all the way around the ruffle strip, taking care not to sew through the thread.*

Step 7 With right sides together, pin the ruffle to the pillow top, matching the quarter points of the ruffle to the corners of the pillow. Pin in place.

Step 8 Gently pull the gathering stitches until the ruffle fits the pillow top, taking care to allow a little extra ruffle at each corner for a full look. Pin in place, and machine baste the ruffle to the pillow top, using a 1/4-inch seam allowance.

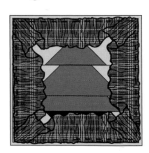

Pillow Back

Cutting

From **TAN PRINT**:
  • Cut 2, 16-1/2 x 20-inch rectangles.

Assembling the Pillow Back

Step 1 With wrong sides together, fold the 16-1/2 x 20-inch **TAN PRINT** rectangles in half to form 2, 10 x 16-1/2-inch double-thick pillow back pieces.

Step 2 Overlap the 2 folded edges by about 4-inches so that the pillow back measures 16-1/2-inches square, and pin. Stitch around the entire pillow back to create a single pillow back.

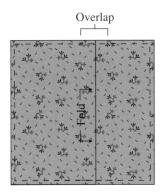

Step 3 With right sides together, layer the pillow back and the pillow top, and pin. The ruffle will be turned toward the center of the pillow at this time. Stitch around the outside edge, using a 3/8-inch seam allowance.

Step 4 Trim the pillow back and corner seam allowances if needed. Turn the pillow right side out and fluff up the ruffle. Insert the pillow form through the back opening.

Christmas Blossom Quilt

Pieced Blocks

Make 4 Blocks

Cutting

From **CREAM PRINT**:
- Cut 2, 3-1/2 x 42-inch strips. From these strips cut 16, 3-1/2-inch squares.
- Cut 1, 6-1/2 x 42-inch strip. From this strip cut: 4, 6-1/2-inch squares.

From **WHEAT PRINT**:
- Cut 3, 3-1/2-inch x 42-inch strips. From these strips cut: 16, 3-1/2 x 6-1/2-inch rectangles.

Piecing

Step 1   Sew 3-1/2 x 6-1/2-inch **WHEAT PRINT** rectangles to both sides of the 6-1/2-inch **CREAM** squares, and press.

Step 2   Sew 3-1/2-inch **CREAM PRINT** squares to both sides of the remaining 3-1/2 x 6-1/2-inch **WHEAT PRINT** rectangles, and press.

FABRICS & SUPPLIES

Finished Size: 43-inches square

Yardage is based on 42-inch wide fabric

1/2 yard **CREAM PRINT** for pieced block

1/2 yard **WHEAT PRINT** for pieced block

1-1/8 yards **RED PRINT** for flower appliqués, lattice pieces, middle border, and corner squares

1/2 yard **GREEN PRINT** for stem appliqués, lattice post, inner border, and corner squares

1/8 yard **BLACK PRINT** for flower center appliqués

1 yard **GREEN PLAID** for outer border

Freezer paper for flower petal appliqués

Step 3 Sew Step 2 units to both sides of the Step 1 units, and press. The blocks should measure 12-1/2-inches square.

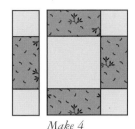

Make 4

Appliquéing the Pieced Blocks

Cutting

From **GREEN PRINT**:
- Cut 2, 1-3/8 x 42-inch strips.

Appliquéing the Stems

Step 1 Fold the **GREEN PRINT** strips in half lengthwise with wrong sides together and press. To keep the raw edges aligned, stitch a scant 1/4-inch away from the raw edges. Fold the strips in half again so the raw edges are hidden by the first folded edge, and press. Cut the strips into 8, 10-1/2-inch-long strips.

Tip: Lynette suggests laying the quilt block on a flat surface for pinning and basting the stems in place. This will help the stems stay nice and flat. Also, basting the stems makes appliquéing so much easier; no pins to catch your thread or prick your fingers.

Step 2 Position the **GREEN PRINT** strips on the quilt block, referring to the Quilt Diagram. Pin and baste the stems in place. Using matching thread, appliqué the stems to the blocks.

Using Freezer Paper Appliqué for Flower Petals

With this appliqué method, the freezer paper forms a base around which the fabric is shaped.

The flower petals are appliquéd using this method. The freezer paper shapes can be reused.

Step 1 Lay the freezer paper, noncoated side up, over the petal shape. With a pencil, trace the petal several times and cut out the shapes.

Step 2 With a dry iron on the wool setting, press the coated side of the freezer paper shapes on the wrong side of the designated fabric. Allow 1/2-inch between each shape. You will need 64 petals for the pieced blocks.

Step 3 Cut out each appliqué shape a scant 1/4-inch beyond the freezer paper edge. Finger press the fabric seam allowance around the edge of the freezer paper.

Step 4 Lightly mark the midpoint on the sides of each 6-inch **BEIGE PRINT** square in the pieced blocks. Marking the squares in this way will help you position the tip of the flower petals.

Step 5 Referring to the Quilt Diagram, pin the petals to the quilt blocks. Position the 4 petals on each block center so that they are 1/8-inch in from the seam line. The petals will overlap a bit at the center, so trim away about 3/8-inch from the overlapping tips.

Step 6 Hand-appliqué the petals in place, using matching thread. When there is about 1/2-inch left to appliqué, remove the freezer paper. To do this, slide your needle into this opening to loosen the freezer paper from the fabric. Gently pull the freezer paper out. Finish stitching the appliqué in place.

Step 7 Appliqué the flower centers to the quilt block, referring to Cardboard Appliqué.

Using Cardboard Appliqué for Flower Centers

With this appliqué method, the cardboard forms a base around which the flower centers are shaped. This technique helps you create smooth, round circles.

Step 1   Make a cardboard template using the flower center shape.

Step 2   Position the template on the wrong side of the **BLACK PRINT** fabric. Trace 20 flower centers, leaving 3/4-inch between each shape. Remove the template and cut a scant 1/4-inch beyond the drawn line of each circle.

Step 3   Run gathering stitches halfway between the drawn line and the cut edge of each circle. The thread ends should be about 3-inches longer than needed.

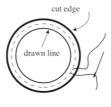

Step 4   Position the cardboard template on the wrong side of a fabric circle. Pull up the gathering stitches. Once the thread is tight, space the gathering evenly, and press. Knot the thread and remove the cardboard template. Repeat to make a total of 20 flower centers.

Step 5   With matching thread, appliqué the flower centers to the flowers.

Step 6   To press the complete appliqué, place the quilt block face down on a towel. Press gently with a dry iron. Pressing in this manner prevents the appliqué shapes from flattening out.

Quilt Center

Cutting

From RED PRINT:

- Cut 2, 2-1/2 x 42-inch strips.

From these strips cut:
4, 2-1/2 x 12-1/2-inch lattice pieces.

From GREEN PRINT:

- Cut 5, 2-1/2-inch squares. One square will be used for the center lattice post, the remaining squares will be used in the middle border as corner squares.

Assembling the Quilt Center

Step 1   Referring to the Quilt Diagram, sew appliquéd blocks to both sides of 2, 2-1/2 x 12-1/2-inch **RED PRINT** lattice pieces, and press.

Step 2   Sew 2-1/2 x 12-1/2-inch **RED PRINT** lattice pieces to both sides of the 2-1/2-inch **GREEN PRINT** lattice post, and press.

Step 3   Sew the Step 1 units to both sides of the lattice strip, and press.

Borders

Note: The yardage given allows for the border strips to be cut on the crosswise grain. Diagonally piece the strips as needed.

Cutting

From GREEN PRINT:

- Cut 4, 1-1/2 x 42-inch inner border strips.

From RED PRINT:

- Cut 4, 2-1/2 x 42-inch middle border strips.
- Cut 4, 6-inch corner squares.

From GREEN PLAID:

- Cut 4, 6 x 42-inch outer border strips.

Attaching the Borders

Step 1   For the inner border, measure the quilt from left to right through the middle to determine the length of the top and bottom borders. Cut 2, 1-1/2-inch wide **GREEN PRINT** strips to this length. Sew the borders to the quilt and press.

Step 2   Measure the quilt from top to bottom through the middle to determine the length of the side borders. Cut 2, 1-1/2-inch wide **GREEN PRINT** strips to this length. Sew the borders to the quilt, and press.

Step 3   For the middle border, measure the quilt as in Step 1 for the inner border. Cut 2, 2-1/2-inch wide **RED PRINT** strips to this length. Sew the borders to the top and bottom of the quilt, and press.

Step 4   Measure the quilt from top to bottom, not including the borders just added. Add 1/2-inch for seam allowances. Cut 2, 2-1/2-inch wide **RED PRINT** strips to this length. Sew 2-1/2-inch **GREEN PRINT** corner squares to both ends of the border strips. Sew the borders to the sides of the quilt, and press.

Step 5   For the outer border, measure the quilt as in Step 1 for the inner border. Cut 2, 6-inch wide **GREEN PLAID** strips to this length. Sew the borders to the top and bottom of the quilt, and press.

Step 6   Measure the quilt as in Step 4. Cut 2, 6-inch wide **GREEN PLAID** strips to this length. Sew 6-inch **RED PRINT** corner squares to both ends of the border strips. Sew the borders to the sides of the quilt, and press.

Putting It All Together

Step 1   Cut the 2-2/3 yard length of **BACKING FABRIC** in half crosswise to form 2, 1-1/3 yard lengths. Remove the selvages and sew the 2 lengths together, and press. Trim the backing and batting so they are 4-inches larger than the quilt top.

Step 2   Mark the quilt top for quilting. Layer the backing, batting, and quilt top. Baste these layers together and quilt.

Step 3   When the quilting is complete, hand baste the layers together a scant 1/4-inch from the raw edge. This hand basting keeps the layers from shifting and prevents puckers from forming when adding the binding. Trim excess batting and backing even with the edge of the quilt top.

Binding

Cutting

From **BLACK PRINT**:
- Cut 5, 2-3/4 x 42-inch strips.

Step 1   Diagonally piece the strips together. Fold the strip in half lengthwise, wrong sides together, and press.

Step 2   With raw edges of the binding and quilt top even, stitch with a 3/8-inch seam allowance.

Step 3   Miter binding at the corners. To do so, stop sewing 3/8-inch from the corner of the quilt. Flip the binding strip up and away from the quilt, then fold the binding down even with the raw edge of the quilt. Begin sewing at the upper edge. Miter all 4 corners in this

manner.

Step 4   Bring the folded edge of the binding to the back of the quilt and hand sew the binding in place.

Flower Center

Trace 20

Petal

Trace 64 onto freezer paper

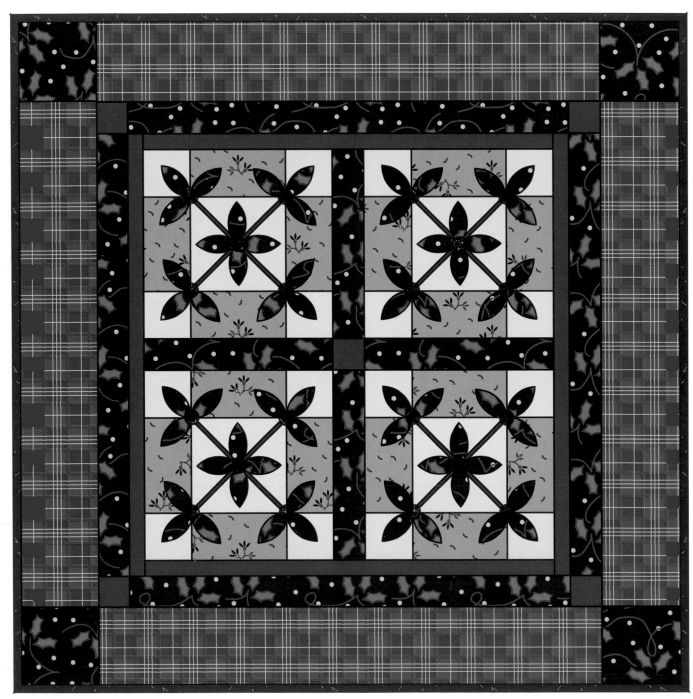

Christmas Blossom Quilt

soft comforts
Winter Warmers

To fill a bedroom with soft comfort, Lynette is certain that you just can't have too many quilts. Keeping them within easy reach of a chair or the bed makes the room a welcoming retreat for family and holiday guests alike.

Back Home Coverlet

Log Cabin Block

Make 30 Blocks

Cutting

From GOLD PRINT:
- Cut 3, 3-1/2 x 42-inch strips.
  From these strips cut:
  30, 3-1/2-inch squares.
- Cut 18, 2 x 42-inch strips.
  From these strips cut: 360, 2-inch squares.

From BLACK PRINT:
- Cut 6, 2 x 42-inch strips.
  From these strips cut:
  60, 2 x 3-1/2-inch rectangles.
- Cut 10, 2 x 42-inch strips.
  From these strips cut:
  60, 2 x 6-1/2-inch rectangles.

From GREEN PRINT:
- Cut 10, 2 x 42-inch strips.
  From these strips cut:
  60, 2 x 6-1/2-inch rectangles.
- Cut 15, 2 x 42-inch strips.
  From these strips cut:
  60, 2 x 9-1/2-inch rectangles.

From RED PRINT:
- Cut 15, 2 x 42-inch strips.
  From these strips cut:
  60, 2 x 9-1/2-inch rectangles.
- Cut 20, 2 x 42-inch strips.
  From these strips cut:
  60, 2 x 12-1/2-inch rectangles.

Assembling the Log Cabin Blocks

Step 1   Sew a 2 x 3-1/2-inch
          BLACK PRINT rectangle
          to both sides of a 3-1/2-inch
          GOLD PRINT square.
          Press seam allowances
          toward the **BLACK
          PRINT** fabric.

Make 30

FABRICS & SUPPLIES

Finished Size: 81 x 95-inches

Yardage is based on 42-inch wide fabric

1-3/4 yards **GOLD PRINT** for centers, triangles, and lattice posts

1-5/8 yards **BLACK PRINT** for log cabin strips and inner border

4-1/4 yards **GREEN PRINT** for log cabin strips, lattice, and outer border

2-1/4 yards **RED PRINT** for log cabin strips

7/8 yard **GOLD PRINT** for binding

5-5/8 yards **BACKING FABRIC**

Quilt batting, at least 85 x 99-inches

A rotary cutter, mat, and wide clear plastic ruler with 1/8-inch markings.

Step 2   Position a 2-inch **GOLD PRINT** square
on the corners of a 2 x 6-1/2-inch
BLACK PRINT rectangle. Draw a
diagonal line from corner to corner
on the **GOLD PRINT** squares.
Stitch on the lines. Trim away corners
leaving a scant 1/4-inch seam allowance.
Press seam allowances toward the
BLACK PRINT fabric.

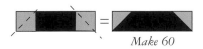

Make 60

Step 3   Sew a unit from Step 2 to the top and
bottom of the Step 1 unit. Press seam
allowances toward the **BLACK PRINT**
fabric. At this point the block should
measure 6-1/2-inches square.

Make 30

Step 4   Sew a 2 x 6-1/2-inch **GREEN PRINT**
rectangle to both sides of the block.
Press seam allowances toward the
GREEN PRINT fabric.

Step 5   Position a 2-inch **GOLD PRINT**
square on the corners of a 2 x 9-1/2-inch
GREEN PRINT rectangle. Draw a
diagonal line from corner to corner on
the **GOLD PRINT** squares. Stitch on
the lines. Trim away corners leaving a
scant 1/4-inch seam allowance. Press
seam allowances toward the **GREEN
PRINT** fabric.

Make 60

Step 6   Sew a unit from Step 5 to the top and
bottom of the block. Press seam
allowances toward the **GREEN PRINT**
fabric. At this point the block should
measure 9-1/2-inches square.

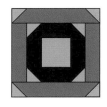

Step 7   Sew a 2 x 9-1/2-inch **RED PRINT**
rectangle to both sides of the block.
Press seam allowances toward the
RED PRINT fabric.

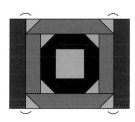

Step 8   Position a 2-inch **GOLD PRINT** square
on the corners of a 2 x 12-1/2-inch
RED PRINT rectangle. Draw a
diagonal line from corner to corner
on the **GOLD PRINT** squares. Stitch
on the line. Trim away corners leaving a
scant 1/4-inch seam allowance. Press
seam allowances toward the **RED
PRINT** fabric.

Make 60

Step 9   Sew a unit from Step 8 to the top
and bottom of the block. Press seam
allowances toward the **RED PRINT**
fabric. At this point the block should
measure 12-1/2-inches square.

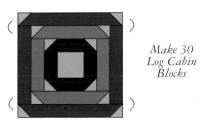

*Make 30
Log Cabin
Blocks*

Quilt Center

Cutting

From **GREEN PRINT**:
- Cut 24, 2 x 42-inch strips.
  From these strips cut:
  71, 2 x 12-1/2-inch lattice strips.

From **GOLD PRINT**:
- Cut 3, 2 x 42-inch strips.
  From these strips cut:
  42, 2-inch squares for lattice posts.

Assembling the Quilt Center

Step 1 Assemble the lattice strips. Each strip is made up of 5, 2 x 12-1/2-inch **GREEN PRINT** strips and 6, 2-inch **GOLD PRINT** lattice posts. Sew the strips and lattice posts together. Press seam allowances toward the **GREEN PRINT** fabric.

Make 7

Step 2 Sew 5 log cabin blocks and 6 **GREEN PRINT** lattice strips together to form each block row. Press seam allowances toward the **GREEN PRINT** fabric. At this point each row should measure 69-1/2-inches long.

Make 6

Step 3 Pin the block rows to the lattice strips. Sew the block rows and lattice strips together to make the quilt center. Press seam allowances toward the lattice strips. At this point the quilt center should measure 69-1/2- x 83-inches.

Borders

Note: The yardage given allows for the border strips to be cut on the crosswise grain. Diagonally piece the strips as needed.

Cutting

From **BLACK PRINT**:
- Cut 8, 2 x 42-inch strips for inner border.

From **GREEN PRINT**:
- Cut 9, 5 x 42-inch strips for outer border.

Attaching the Borders

Step 1 For the inner border, measure the quilt from left to right, through the middle, to determine the length of the top and bottom borders. Cut 2, 2-inch wide **BLACK PRINT** strips to this length. Sew the borders to the quilt, and press.

Step 2 Measure the quilt from top to bottom, through the middle, to determine the length of the side borders. Cut 2, 2-inch wide **BLACK PRINT** strips to this length. Sew the borders to the quilt, and press.

Step 3 For the outer border, measure the quilt as in Step 1. Cut 2, 5-inch wide **GREEN PRINT** strips to this length. Sew the borders to the top and bottom of the quilt, and press.

Step 4 Measure the quilt as in Step 2. Cut 2, 5-inch wide **GREEN PRINT** strips to this length. Sew the borders to the sides of the quilt, and press.

Putting It All Together

Step 1 Cut the 5-5/8 yard length of **BACKING FABRIC** in half crosswise to make 2, 2-3/4 yard lengths. Trim the backing and batting so they are 4-inches larger than the quilt top.

Step 2 Mark the quilt top for quilting. Layer the backing, batting, and quilt top. Baste the 3 layers together and quilt.

Step 3 When quilting is complete, hand-baste the 3 layers together a scant 1/4-inch from the edge. This hand basting keeps the layers from shifting and prevents puckers from forming when adding the binding. Trim excess batting and backing even with the edge of the quilt top.

Binding

Cutting

From **GOLD PRINT**:

• Cut 9, 2-3/4 x 42-inch strips.

Step 1   Diagonally piece the strips together. Fold the strip in half lengthwise, wrong sides together, and press.

Step 2   With raw edges of the binding and quilt top even, stitch with a 3/8-inch seam allowance.

Step 3   Miter binding at the corners. To do so, stop sewing 3/8-inch from the corner of the quilt. Flip the binding strip up and away from the quilt, then fold the binding down even with the raw edge of the quilt. Begin sewing at the upper edge. Miter all 4 corners in this manner.

Step 4   Bring the folded edge of the binding to the back of the quilt and hand sew the binding in place.

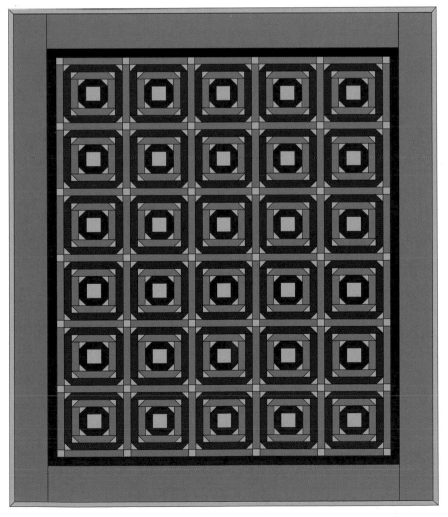

Back Home Coverlet

Gift-giving has never been easier with new packaging options like rubber stamps and unpainted papier-maché boxes inspired by antiques like the church ornament shown on the following page. Lynette discovered the tiny 2-inch treasure in a box of ornaments purchased at an auction.

For small gifts, use stacking star boxes decorated with holly and glitter. Paint the gift boxes for a galaxy of stars.

For a special Christmas tree table favor that will become the star attraction of any holiday table, cut two cookies each using five sizes of star-shaped cutters, then bake the cookies and stack them up—secured with a bit of frosting for incredible edibles!

A small wall quilt is always a "must" on Lynette's Christmas gift list. She uses simple appliqué shapes like stars, snowflakes, and pine trees and rotary-cut strip piecing to quickly make several at a time.

Christmas Snow Wall Quilt

FABRICS & SUPPLIES

Finished Size: 24 x 32-inches

Yardage is based on 42-inch wide fabric

5/8 yard **BEIGE PRINT**
for background and checkerboard

1/4 yard **BLACK PRINT** for checkerboard

7 x 10-inch rectangle **GREEN PRINT #1**
for large tree appliqué

9 x 11-inch rectangle **GREEN PRINT #2**
for small tree appliqué

12-inch square **CREAM PRINT**
for snowflake appliqués

1/3 yard **RED PRINT** for inner border

3/8 yard **BROWN PRINT** for outer border

1/2 yard paper-backed fusible web

1/3 yard **BLACK PRINT** for binding

---

1 yard **BACKING FABRIC**

Quilt batting, at least 28 x 36-inches

#8 black perle cotton

A rotary cutter, mat, and wide clear
plastic ruler with 1/8-inch markings

Quilt Center

Cutting

From BEIGE PRINT:
- Cut 1, 14-1/2 x 16-1/2-inch rectangle
  for background.
- Cut 1, 2-1/2 x 42-inch strip for
  checkerboard.

From BLACK PRINT:
- Cut 1, 2-1/2 x 42-inch strip.
  From this strip cut one 2-1/2-inch square.
  The remainder of the strip will be used for
  checkerboard strip piecing.

From RED PRINT:
- Cut 2, 2-1/2 x 14-1/2-inch strips and 2,
  2-1/2 x 26-1/2-inch strips for inner border.

From BROWN PRINT:
- Cut 3, 3-1/2 x 42-inch strips for outer
  border. Diagonally piece the strips as needed.

Piecing

Step 1   Aligning long edges, sew the
2-1/2 x 42-inch **BEIGE PRINT** and
BLACK PRINT strips together,
and press. Refer to page 202 for
Hints and Helps for Pressing Strip Sets.
Cut the strip set into segments.

Crosscut 10, 2-1/2-inch wide segments

Step 2   Sew 7, Step 1 segments together, side to side, and press.

Step 3   Sew 3 segments together, end to end, and press. Add a 2-1/2-inch **BLACK PRINT** square to the end, and press.

Step 4   Sew the Step 3 strip to the bottom of the Step 2 strip, and press. At this point the checkerboard unit should measure 6-1/2 x 14-1/2-inches.

Step 5   Sew the 14-1/2 x 16-1/2-inch **BEIGE PRINT** rectangle to the top of the checkerboard, and press.

Step 6   Sew the 2-1/2 x 14-1/2-inch **RED PRINT** strips to the top and bottom of the quilt, and press.

Step 7   Sew the 2-1/2 x 26-1/2-inch **RED PRINT** strips to the sides of the quilt, and press.

Step 8   Stay-stitch a scant 1/4-inch from the outside edges to stabilize the quilt before adding the appliqué.

Fusible Appliqué

Step 1   Read and follow the manufacturer's directions for the fusible web.

Step 2   Trace the appliqué designs (found on the following pages) onto the paper side of the fusible web, leaving 1/2-inch between each shape. Cut around each traced shape, roughly 1/4-inch outside of the traced line.

Step 3   Following manufacturer's directions, fuse each shape to the wrong side of the designated appliqué fabrics. Cut out each

shape on the drawn line and peel away the backing paper.

Step 4   Arrange the appliqué shapes on the quilt top, referring to the quilt diagram. The trees should be placed 1/4-inch above the checkerboard. The center snowflake should extend 1-inch into the top inner border. The side snowflakes should be 2-1/2-inches from the top of the **BEIGE PRINT** background piece and should extend 3/4-inch into the side inner borders. When everything is in position, fuse in place.

Step 5   With black perle cotton, buttonhole-stitch around the appliqué shapes.

Outer Border

Step 1   Measure the quilt from left to right, through the middle, to determine the length of the top and bottom borders. Cut 2, 3-1/2-inch wide **BROWN PRINT** strips to this measurement. Sew the borders to the quilt, and press.

Step 2   Measure the quilt from top to bottom, through the middle, to determine the length of the side borders. Cut 2, 3-1/2-inch wide **BROWN PRINT** strips to this measurement. Sew the borders to the quilt, and press.

Putting It All Together

Step 1   Trim the **BACKING FABRIC** and batting so they are 4-inches larger than the quilt top.

Step 2   Mark the quilt top for quilting. Layer the backing, batting, and quilt top. Baste the 3 layers together and quilt.

Step 3   When the quilting is complete, hand-baste the 3 layers together a scant 1/4-inch from the raw edge.

This hand basting keeps the layers from shifting and prevents puckers from forming when adding the binding.

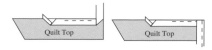

Trim excess batting and backing even with the edge of the quilt top.

Binding

Cutting

From **BLACK PRINT**:
  • Cut 4, 2-3/4 x 42-inch strips.

Step 1

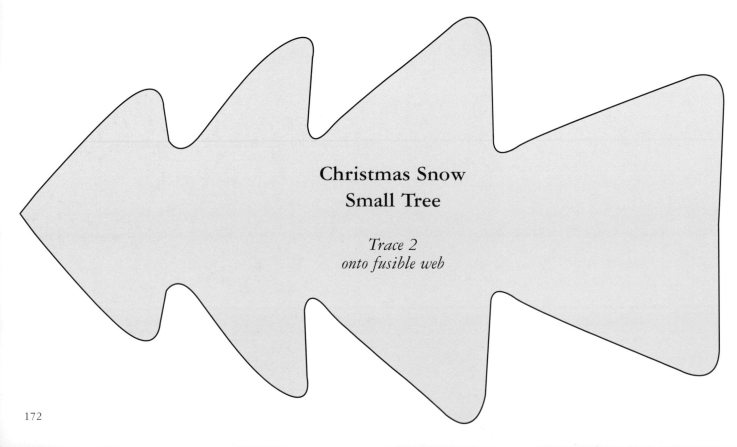

**Christmas Snow
Small Tree**

*Trace 2
onto fusible web*

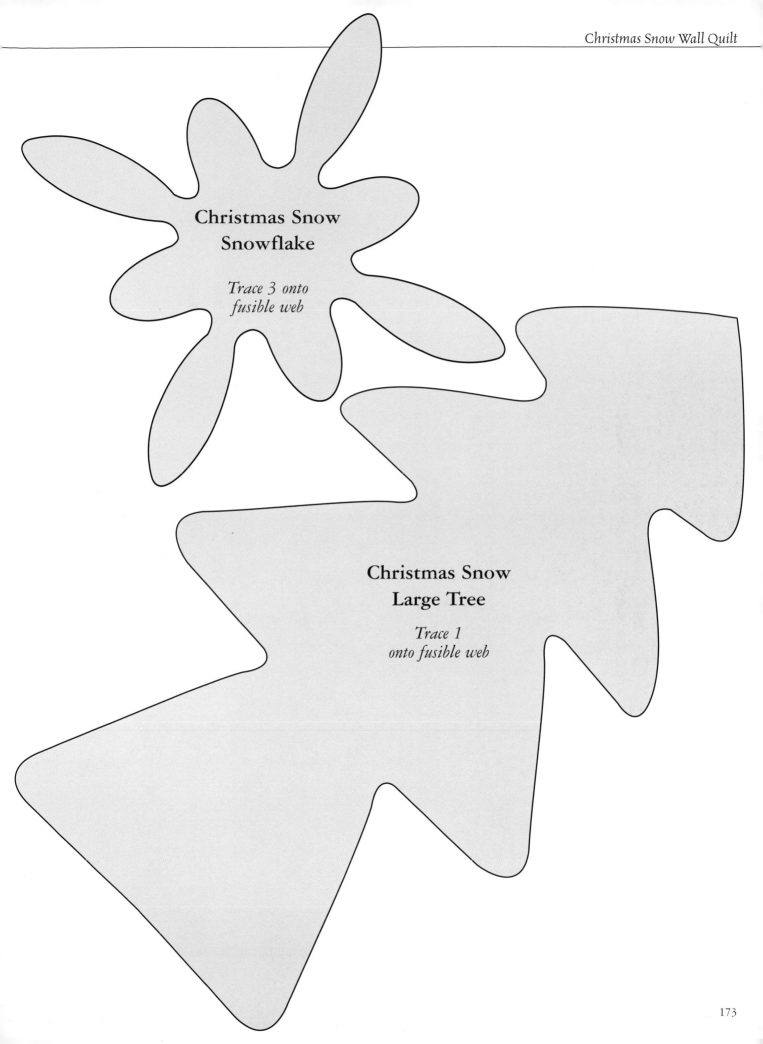

**Christmas Snow
Snowflake**

*Trace 3 onto
fusible web*

**Christmas Snow
Large Tree**

*Trace 1
onto fusible web*

Each year Lynette

tries to find new and

creative ways to make

the presentation as

interesting as

the gift itself.

A beautifully-wrapped

gift offers no clue

to its contents, but it

does say a lot about

the giver, right down

to the gift tag.

Star & Heart Ornaments

In early December a small forest suddenly springs up on the sidewalk leading to our home.
I purchase several dozen of these tabletop-sized trees from the local nursery to give as gifts.
Departing guests each choose an ornament-topped tree as a special treat to enjoy at home.

FABRICS & SUPPLIES

11-inch square of
COTTON FABRIC for front

2, 11-inch squares of **BLACK WOOL**
fabric for front edging and backing

Perle cotton or embroidery floss
(a contrasting color and black)

Large button for decoration

Paper-backed fusible web for appliqué

Fiberfill for stuffing

1/3 yard of 3/4-inch-wide
grosgrain ribbon for tree topper

1/2 yard of 1/4-inch-wide
grosgrain ribbon for ornament

Makes one ornament

Step 1 Trace the shape (found on the following pages) onto the paper side of the fusible web. Press the shape to the wrong side of the fabric chosen for the tree topper/ornament. Cut out the shape directly on the traced outline. Peel off the paper backing.

Step 2 With a hot dry iron fuse the shape to one of the wool squares. Cut out, allowing 3/8-inch of the wool to extend beyond the appliqué edge.

Step 3 With contrasting perle cotton, buttonhole-stitch the appliqué to the wool. Stem-stitch the lines on the star. See page 202 for the Decorative Stitch diagrams.

Step 4 With wrong sides together, layer the appliquéd shape onto the second piece of wool. Using the appliquéd shape as a pattern, cut the second piece of wool to this size.

Step 5 With perle cotton, buttonhole-stitch the raw edges of the 2 layers of wool together, leaving 2 inches open for stuffing the shape. Stop stitching, but do not tie off the thread at this point.

Step 6 Fill the shape sparingly with fiberfill to create a slight puff. Continue buttonhole stitching to finish.

Step 7 With a double strand of perle cotton, stitch the large button to the shape as shown in the photograph. The threads should go all the way to the backside. Pull the threads tightly to nestle the button into the puffy shape and knot the threads.

Step 8 To finish the tree topper, fold the 12-inch length of 3/4-inch-wide grosgrain ribbon in half crosswise. Hand-stitch the folded edge to the center back of the tree topper; tie it to the tree.

Step 9 To finish the ornament, fold the 18-inch length of 1/4-inch-wide grosgrain ribbon in half crosswise. Hand-stitch the folded edge to the top of the ornament; tie with an overhand knot.

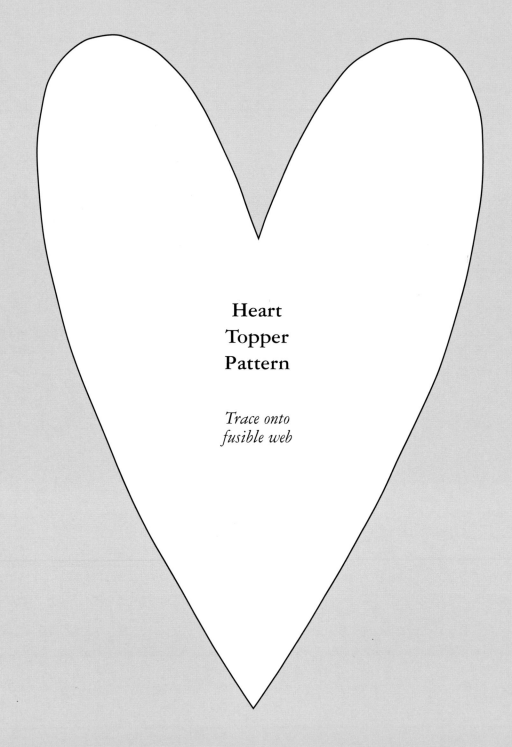

**Heart
Topper
Pattern**

*Trace onto
fusible web*

**Star
Topper
Pattern**

*Trace onto
fusible web*

Gingerbread Candle Holders

Just inside the back entrance, even the hallway is a welcome sight. Lynette fills the wall with a handsome pine cupboard lined with mixing bowls which she rearranges seasonally. At Christmastime her collection features Yellowware, green and caramel bowls brimming with artificial sugar-frosted fruit, pomegranates, and greens interspersed with home-made gingerbread houses and star cookie-cutter candle holders.

To make the candle holders, use the basic gingerbread recipe provided on the following page. (Vary the color of the gingerbread by substituting dark molasses for light molasscs.)

Gingerbread House

Roll cookie dough to 1/4-inch thickness. Cut out house shapes. Using a star cookie cutter, cut a star cookie for front of house. Bake on lightly greased cookie sheets at 375° for 10 minutes. Baking time may vary depending on thickness of cookies. Cool completely before assembling.

Make a very stiff frosting using powdered sugar and water. Frost edges of house sides and attach to house front and back. Prop house sections with canned goods until frosting has dried completely. Frost edges of one side of the house and place one roof section on that side of the house. Hold in place until frosting is dry enough so roof does not slide off house. When dry, frost edge of roof already on house and the remaining house edges, and place second roof section on house. Adding extra frosting to the eaves of the house makes it look like you've added a dusting of snow!

Gingerbread

1 cup shortening

1 cup granulated sugar

1 cup light (or dark) molasses

1 T. vinegar

2 slightly beaten eggs

5 1/2 cups flour

1 tsp. cinnamon

1 tsp. ginger

1 tsp. soda

1/2 tsp. salt

Combine shortening, sugar, molasses and vinegar in a 2-quart saucepan. Bring slowly to a boil. Remove from heat, cool to room temperature. Add eggs to cooled mixture.

Mix flour, cinnamon, ginger, soda, and salt together and stir into the molasses mixture until dough is smooth and satiny. (At this point, dough is extremely soft, but it firms up when it is refrigerated.)

Divide into two portions. Wrap in plastic wrap and chill for at least two hours. (Can be refrigerated for several days if necessary.) Let stand at room temperature a few minutes until it is pliable enough to roll.

Gingerbread Candle Holders

Cut 3 star cookies from gingerbread dough for each candle holder. Cut 1 round cookie for base. Cut a hole from the center of each star cookie a bit larger than the diameter of the candle you are using. Bake on lightly greased cookie sheets at 375° for 10 minutes. Baking time may vary depending on thickness of cookies. Cool completely before assembling candle holders.

Layer star cookies on round cookie base and frost in place. Using a generous amount of frosting, place candle in base and hold upright until frosting is firm and candle stays upright. Hot-glue small berries and pine cones to decorate candle holder.

**Gingerbread
House Pattern**

Side

**Gingerbread
House Pattern**

Front and Back

**Gingerbread
House Pattern**

Roof

Even Lynette's enclosed,

unheated back porch which is

unused during the winter, gets

trimmed in holiday style. Lynette

fills it with favorite summer

collectibles, dried hydrangeas

from her garden, and a red and

green quilt.

Here, the view from the

French doors into the dining room

is of the porch. Tin toys, sand pails,

and the country-blue wardrobe

swagged with mittens and pine

cones, set the scene for a rustic

collection of everything

from stockings to snowshoes.

comfort and joy
Christmas Brunch

For the Christmas brunch tabletop, celebrate naturally by cutting logs into 2-inch thick rounds. Stack several log rounds to use as a base for a glass-shaded candle—the season's symbol of warmth and good cheer.

You're Invited

Inviting ideas for a memorable cottage-style Christmas brunch begin with the festive invitation shown above. Printed on vellum purchased at a stationery store, the invitation is held in place with old-fashioned gold photo corners. A simple pine bough rubber stamp was used to create an all-over pattern for the cover stock background.

Party Favor

Create cottage style—naturally. The gift box party favor shown above can also be used as a place card by adding the guest's name to the star-stenciled slice of pine. To decorate the miniature lidded paper-maché box, begin by painting it deep red and adding white dots of paint applied with the handled end of a small paint brush. Stencil a star in the center of a thin "slice" or round cut from the base of a cleverly recycled Christmas tree. Drill a tiny hole in the tree round and use a piece of wire to tie it tightly to the curling ribbon bow so it stands upright.

Oven French Toast

3 beaten eggs

1-1/2 cups milk

3 T. sugar

1/2 tsp. vanilla

8 slices 1-inch thick French bread

3 T. butter or margarine

Cinnamon and sugar mixture

1/2 cup chopped pecans

Mix first four ingredients. Melt butter and pour evenly on bottom of cookie sheet. Soak 8 pieces of bread, one at a time, in the mixture and place on cookie sheet. Bake at 350° for 15 minutes. Turn bread over and sprinkle with mixture of cinnamon and sugar. Bake an additional 10 minutes or until golden brown. Sprinkle with chopped pecans and maple syrup.

Makes 4 servings.

Holiday Egg Scramble

2 T. vegetable oil

2 T. butter

1 small green pepper, finely chopped

1 bunch green onions, sliced

1 cup finely sliced ham, cut into
   1/4-inch wide strips (5-1/2 ozs.)

4 oz. mushrooms, sliced (1-1/2 cups)

1 lb. 4 oz. package of cooked, sliced home fries

10 beaten eggs

1/4 cup milk

1/4 tsp. salt

1/8 tsp. pepper

1 cup shredded cheddar cheese (4 oz.)

In a 15-inch non-stick skillet, sauté the green pepper, onion, ham and mushrooms in the oil over medium-high heat until soft, stirring occasionally. Cook until the moisture from the mushrooms has evaporated. Set aside.

Add the butter to the same skillet, then the cooked potatoes. Cook and stir occasionally for 8 to 10 minutes or until potatoes are slightly browned.

Combine eggs, milk, salt and pepper. and add to skillet. Reduce heat to medium and cook, stirring occasionally until eggs are just set. Add pepper, onion, ham, and mushroom mixture.

Sprinkle with cheese. Cover and cook without stirring for 3 minutes.

Makes 8–10 servings.

Since the holiday season

can often be hectic,

it's important to have a

quiet retreat to rest,

reflect, and refresh.

In the upstairs of

Lynette's home, each of

the bedrooms has its

own special tree and a

bed piled high with

comforting quilts and

pillows in classic

country colors for sweet

dreams to all.

Fireside Medallion Quilt

1 skein black embroidery floss

1-1/4-inch yards **BACKING FABRIC**

Quilt batting, at least 42-inches square

A rotary cutter, mat, and wide
clear plastic ruler with 1/8-inch markings

Quilt Center
Cutting

From **GOLD PRINT**:
- Cut 1, 2-1/2-inch square for 9-patch block.
- Cut 4, 5-1/2-inch squares for corner squares.

From **BLACK PRINT**:
- Cut 8, 2-1/2-inch squares for 9-patch block and block border.
- Cut 4, 5-1/2 x 42-inch strips for outer border.

From **RED PRINT**:
- Cut 4, 2-1/2-inch squares for 9-patch block.
- Cut 1, 1-1/2 x 42-inch strip for inner border.

From **GREEN PRINT**:
- Cut 4, 2-1/2 x 6-1/2-inch rectangles for block borders.

From **BLACK/BEIGE PLAID**:
- Cut 4, 8 x 42-inch strips for middle border.

Piecing the 9-Patch Block

Step 1   Sew a 2-1/2-inch **RED PRINT** square to both sides of a 2-1/2-inch **BLACK PRINT** square, and press.

 Make 2

Step 2   Sew a 2-1/2-inch **BLACK PRINT** square to both sides of a 2-1/2-inch **GOLD PRINT** square, and press.

 Make 1

FABRICS & SUPPLIES

Finished Size: 38-inches square
Yardage is based on 42-inch wide fabric

1/4 yard **GOLD PRINT**
for center square and corner squares

3/4 yard **BLACK PRINT** for 9-patch block,
block border, and outer border

1/4 yard **RED PRINT** for 9-patch block,
inner border, and circle appliqués

5/8 yard **GREEN PRINT**
for block border and swag appliqués

1 yard **BLACK/BEIGE PLAID**
for middle border

1/2 yard **RED PRINT** for binding

1 yard paper-backed fusible web

Step 3   Sew a Step 1 unit to both sides of a Step 2 unit to form the 9-patch block, and press.

Make 1

Step 4   Sew a 2-1/2 x 6-1/2-inch **GREEN PRINT** block border rectangle to the top and bottom of the 9-patch block, and press.

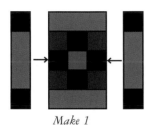

Make 1

Step 5   Add a 2-1/2-inch **BLACK PRINT** square to both ends of the remaining 2-1/2 x 6-1/2-inch **GREEN PRINT** rectangles. Sew the block borders to the sides of the 9-patch block, and press.

Attaching the Borders

Step 1   For the inner border measure the quilt from left to right, through the middle, to determine the length of the top and bottom borders. Cut 2, 1-1/2-inch wide **RED PRINT** strips to this length. Sew the borders to the top and bottom of the quilt, and press.

Step 2   Measure the quilt from top to bottom, through the center, to determine the length of the side borders. Cut 2, 1-1/2-inch wide **RED PRINT** strips to this length. Sew the borders to the sides of the quilt, and press.

Step 3   For the middle border, measure the quilt as in Step 1. Cut 2, 8-inch wide **BLACK/BEIGE PLAID** strips to this length. Sew the borders to the top and bottom of the quilt, and press.

Step 4   Measure the quilt as in Step 2. Cut 2, 8-inch wide **BLACK/BEIGE PLAID** strips to this length. Sew the borders to the sides of the quilt, and press. Stay-stitch a scant 1/4-inch from the raw edges to stabilize the quilt before the quilt is appliquéd.

Adding the Appliqué

Step 1   Position the fusible web over the appliqué patterns, paper side up. Trace 4 pattern A, 4 pattern B, and 16 pattern C, leaving 1/2-inch between each tracing. Cut out the pieces roughly 1/4-inch outside of the traced lines.

Step 2   Press the fusible web shapes onto the back of the fabrics used for the appliqués; let the fabric cool. Cut out the shapes on the drawn lines. Peel off paper backing.

Step 3   Position the appliqué shapes on the quilt. With a hot, dry iron, press in place. With 3 strands of black floss, appliqué the shapes using a buttonhole stitch.

Attaching the Outer Border

Step 1   Measure the quilt as you did for the middle border. Cut 2, 5-1/2 -inch wide **BLACK PRINT** strips to this length. Sew the borders to the top and bottom of the quilt, and press.

Step 2   Measure the quilt from top to bottom, not including the borders just added. Add 1/2-inch for seam allowances. Cut 2, 5-1/2 -inch wide **BLACK PRINT** strips to this length. Sew 5-1/2-inch **GOLD PRINT** corner squares to both ends of the border strips. Sew the borders to the sides of the quilt, and press.

Putting It All Together

Step 1   Trim the **BACKING FABRIC** and batting so they are 4-inches larger than the quilt top.

Step 2   Mark the quilt top for quilting. Layer the backing, batting, and quilt top. Baste the 3 layers together and quilt.

Step 3   When quilting is complete, hand-baste the 3 layers together a scant 1/4-inch from the edge. This hand basting keeps the layers from shifting and prevents puckers from forming when adding the binding. Trim excess batting and backing even with the edge of the quilt top.

Binding

Cutting
From **RED PRINT**:

• Cut 4, 2-3/4 x 42-inch strips.

Step 1   Diagonally piece the strips together. Fold the strips in half lengthwise, wrong sides together, and press.

Step 2   With raw edges of the binding and quilt top even, stitch with a 3/8-inch seam allowance.

Step 3   Miter binding at the corners. To do so, stop sewing 3/8-inch from the corner of the quilt. Flip the binding strip up and away from the quilt, then fold the binding down even with the raw edge of the quilt. Begin sewing at the upper edge. Miter all 4 corners in this manner.

Step 4   Bring the folded edge of the binding to the back of the quilt and hand sew the binding in place.

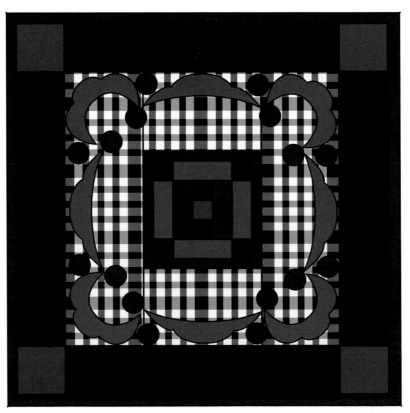

Fireside Medallion Quilt

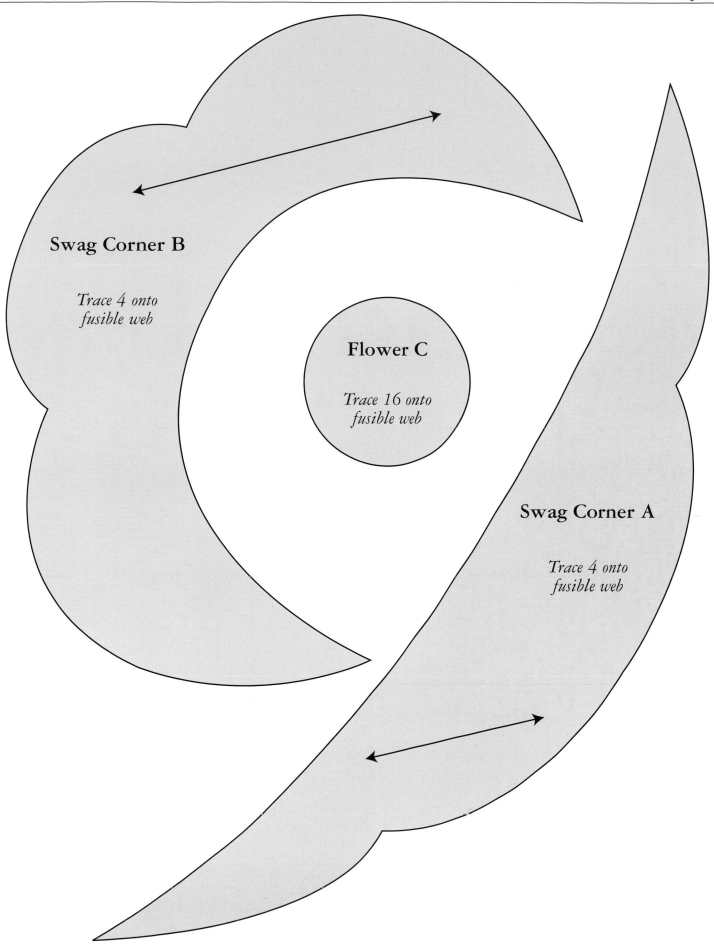

Swag Corner B

*Trace 4 onto
fusible web*

Flower C

*Trace 16 onto
fusible web*

Swag Corner A

*Trace 4 onto
fusible web*

General Instructions

General Instructions

Getting Started

Yardage is based on 42-inch wide fabric. If your fabric is wider or narrower, it will affect the amount of necessary strips you need to cut in some patterns, and of course, it will affect the amount of fabric you have left over. Generally, Thimbleberries® patterns allow for a little extra fabric so you can confidently cut your pattern pieces with ease.

A rotary cutter, mat, and wide clear plastic ruler with 1/8-inch markings are needed tools in attaining accuracy. A beginner needs good tools just as an experienced quilt-maker needs good equipment. A 24 x 36-inch mat board is a good size to own. It will easily accommodate the average quilt fabrics and will aid in accurate cutting. The plastic ruler you purchase should be at least 6 x 24 inches and easy to read. Do not purchase a smaller ruler to save money. The large size will be invaluable to your quilt-making success.

It is often recommended to prewash and press fabrics to test for color fastness and possible shrinkage. If you choose to prewash, wash in cool water and dry in a cool to moderate dryer. Industry standards actually suggest that line drying is best. Shrinkage is generally very minimal and usually is not a concern. A good way to test your fabric for both shrinkage and color fastness is to cut a 3-inch square of fabric. Soak the fabric in a white bowl filled with water. Squeeze the water out of the fabric and press it dry on a piece of muslin. If the fabric is going to release color, it will do so either in the water or when it is pressed dry. Remeasure the 3-inch fabric square to see if it has changed size considerably (more than 1/4 inch). If it has, wash, dry, and press the entire yardage. This little test could save you hours in prewashing and pressing.

Read instructions thoroughly before beginning a project. Each step will make more sense to you when you have a general overview of the whole process. Take one step at a time and follow the illustrations. They will often make more sense to you than the words. Take "baby steps" so you don't get overwhelmed by the entire process.

When working with flannel and other loosely woven fabrics, always prewash and dry. These fabrics almost always shrink more.

For piecing, place right sides of the fabric pieces together and use 1/4-inch seam allowances throughout the entire quilt unless otherwise specifically stated in the directions. An accurate seam allowance is the most important part of the quilt-making process after accurately cutting. All the directions are based on accurate 1/4-inch seam allowances. It is very important to check your sewing machine to see what position your fabric should be to get accurate seams. To test, use a piece of 1/4-inch graph paper, stitch along the quarter inch line as if the paper were fabric. Make note of where the edge of the paper lines up with your presser foot or where it lines up on the throat of the plate of your machine. Many quilters place a piece of masking tape on the throat plate to help guide the edge of the fabric. Now test your seam allowance on fabric. Cut 2, 2-1/2-inch squares, place right sides together and stitch along one edge. Press seam allowances in one direction and measure. At this point the unit should measure 2-1/2 x 4-1/2-inches. If it does not, adjust your stitching guidelines and test again. Seam allowances are included in the cutting sizes given in this book.

Pressing is the third most important step in quilt-making. As a general rule, you should never cross a stitched seam with another seam unless it has been pressed. Therefore, every time you stitch a seam, it needs to be pressed before adding another piece. Often, it will feel like you press as much as you sew, and often that is true. It is very important that you press and not iron the seams. Pressing is a firm, up-and-down motion that will flatten the seams but not distort the piecing. Ironing is a back and forth motion and will stretch and distort the small pieces. Most quilters use steam to help the pressing process. The moisture does help and will not distort the shapes as long as the pressing motion is used.

An old-fashioned rule is to press seam allowances in one direction, toward the darker fabric. Often, background fabrics are light in color and pressing toward the darker fabric prevents the seam allowances from showing through to the right side. Pressing seam allowances in one direction is thought to create a stronger seam. Also, for ease in hand-quilting, the quilting lines should fall on the side of the seam which is opposite the seam allowance. As you piece quilts, you will find these "rules" to be helpful but not neccesarily always appropriate. Sometimes seams need to be pressed in the opposite direction so the seams of different units will fit together more easily, which quilters refer to as seams "nesting" together. When sewing together two units with opposing seam allowances, use the tip of your seam ripper to gently guide the units under your presser foot. Sometimes it is necessary to re-press the seams to make the units fit together nicely. Always try to achieve the least bulk in one spot and accept that no matter which way you press, it may be a little tricky and it could be a little bulky.

Pressing Direction

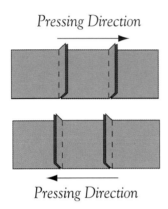

Pressing Direction

Squaring Up Blocks

To square up your blocks, first check the seam allowances. This is usually where the problem is, and it is always best to alter within the block rather than trim the outer edges. Next, make sure you have pressed accurately. Sometimes a block can become distorted by ironing instead of pressing.

To trim up block edges, use one of many clear plastic squares available on the market. Determine the center of the block; mark with a pin. Lay the square over the block and align as many perpendicular and horizontal lines as you can to the seams in your block. This will indicate where the block is off.

Do not trim all off on one side; this usually results in real distortion of the pieces in the block and the block design. Take a little off all sides until the block is square. When assembling many blocks, it is necessary to make sure all are the same size.

Tools and Equipment

Making beautiful quilts does not require a large number of specialized tools or expensive equipment. My list of favorites is short and sweet and includes the things I

use over and over again because they are always accurate and dependable.

I find a long acrylic ruler indispensable for accurate rotary cutting. The ones I like most are an Omnigrid 6 x 24-inch grid acrylic ruler for cutting long strips and squaring up fabrics and quilt tops and a Masterpiece 45, 8 x 24-inch ruler for cutting 6- to 8-inch wide borders. I sometimes tape together two 6 x 24-inch acrylic rulers for cutting borders up to 12 inches wide.

A 15-inch Omnigrid square acrylic ruler is great for squaring up individual blocks and corners of a quilt top, for cutting strips up to 15 inches wide or long, and for trimming side and corner triangles.

I think the markings on my 23 x 35-inch Olfa rotary cutting mat stay visible longer than on other mats, and the lines are fine and accurate.

The largest size Olfa rotary cutter cuts through many layers of fabric easily, and it isn't cumbersome to use. The 2-1/2-inch blade slices through three layers of backing, batting, and a quilt top like butter.

An 8-inch pair of Gingher shears is great for cutting out appliqué templates and cutting fabric from a bolt or fabric scraps.

I keep a pair of 5-1/2-inch Gingher scissors by my sewing machine so it is handy for both machine work and hand-work. This size is versatile and sharp enough to make large and small cuts equally well.

My Grabbit magnetic pin cushion has a surface that is large enough to hold lots of straight pins and a strong magnet that keeps them securely in place.

Silk pins are long and thin, which means they won't leave large holes in your fabric. I like them because they increase accuracy in pinning pieces or blocks together and it is easy to press over silk pins as well.

For pressing individual pieces, blocks, and quilt tops, I use an 18 x 48-inch sheet of plywood covered with several layers of cotton fiberfill and topped with a layer of muslin stapled to the back. The 48-inch length allows me to press an entire width of fabric at one time without the need to reposition it, and the square ends are better than tapered ends on an ironing board for pressing finished quilt tops.

Rotary Cutting

SAFETY FIRST! The blades of a rotary cutter are very sharp and need to be for accurate cutting. Look at a variety of cutters to find one that feels good in your hand. All quality cutters have a safety mechanism to "close" the cutting blade when not in use. After each cut and before laying the rotary cutter down, close the blade. Soon this will become second nature to you and will prevent dangerous accidents. Always keep cutters out of the sight of children. Rotary cutters are very tempting to fiddle with when they are lying around. When your blade is dull or nicked, change it. Damaged blades do not cut accurately and require extra effort that can also result in slipping and injury. Also, always cut away from yourself for safety.

Fold the fabric in half lengthwise matching the selvage edges.

"Square off" the ends of your fabric before measuring and cutting pieces. This means that the cut edge of the fabric must be exactly perpendicular to the folded edge which creates a 90° angle. Align the folded and selvage edges of the fabric with the lines on the cutting board, and place a ruled square on the fold. Place a 6 x 24-inch ruler against the side of the square to get a 90° angle. Hold the ruler in place, remove the square, and cut along the edge of the ruler. If you are left-handed, work from the other end of the fabric. Use the lines on your cutting board to help line up fabric, but not to measure and cut strips. Use a ruler for accurate cutting, always checking to make sure your fabric is lined up with horizontal and vertical lines on the ruler.

6 x 24-inch ruler

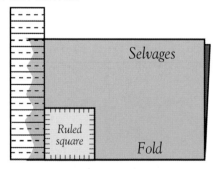

Cutting Strips

When cutting strips or rectangles, cut on the crosswise grain. Strips can then be cut into squares or smaller rectangles.

If your strips are not straight after cutting a few of them, refold the fabric, align the folded and selvage edges with the lines on the cutting board, and "square off" the edge again by trimming to straighten, and begin cutting.

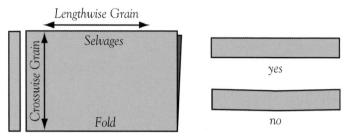

Trimming Side and Corner Triangles

Begin at a corner by lining up your ruler 1/4-inch beyond the points of the corners of the blocks as shown.

Cut along the edge of the ruler. Repeat this procedure on all four sides of the quilt top.

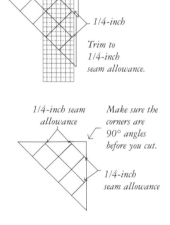

Helpful Hints for Sewing with Flannel

Always prewash and machine dry flannel. This will prevent severe shrinkage after the quilt is made. Some flannels shrink more than others. For this reason, we have allowed approximately 1/4 yard extra for each fabric under the fabric requirements. Treat the more heavily napped side of solid flannels as the right side of the fabric.

Because flannel stretches more than other cotton calicos and because the nap makes them thicker, the quilt design should be simple. Let the fabric and color make the design statement.

Consider combining regular cotton calicos with flannels. The different textures complement each other nicely.

Use a 10 to 12 stitches per inch setting on your machine.

A 1/4-inch seam allowance is also recommended for flannel piecing.

When sewing triangle-pieced squares together, take extra care not to stretch the diagonal seam. Trim off the points from the seam allowances to eliminate bulk.

Press gently to prevent stretching pieces out of shape.

Check block measurements as you progress. "Square up" the blocks as needed. Flannel will shift and it is easy to end up with blocks that are misshapen. If you trim and measure as you go, you are more likely to have accurate blocks. If you notice a piece of flannel is stretching more than the others, place it on the bottom when stitching on the machine. The natural action of the feed dogs will help prevent it from stretching.

Before stitching pieces, strips, or borders together, pin often to prevent fabric from stretching and moving. When stitching longer pieces together, divide the pieces into quarters and pin. Divide into even smaller sections to get more control.

Use a lightweight batting to prevent the quilt from becoming too heavy.

Cutting Triangles from Squares

Cutting accurate triangles can be intimidating for beginners, but a clear plastic ruler, rotary cutter, and cutting mat are all that are needed to make perfect triangles. The cutting instructions often direct you to cut strips, then squares, and then triangles.

Sewing Layered Strips Together

When you are instructed to layer strips, right sides together, and sew, you need to take some precautions. Gently lay a strip on top of another, carefully lining up the raw edges. Pressing the strips together will hold them together nicely, and a few pins here and there will also help. Be careful not to stretch the strips as you sew them together.

Rod Casing or Sleeve to Hang Quilts

To hang wall quilts, attach a casing that is made of the same fabric as the quilt back. Attach this casing at the top of the quilt, just below the binding. Often, it is helpful to attach a second casing at the bottom of the quilt so you can insert a dowel into it which will help weight the quilt and make it hang free of ripples.

To make a rod casing or "sleeve," cut enough strips of fabric equal to the width of the quilt plus 2 inches for side hems. Generally, 6-inch wide strips will accommodate most rods. If you are using a rod with a larger diameter, increase the width of the strips.

Seam the strips together to get the length needed; press. Fold the strip in half lengthwise, wrong sides together. Stitch the long raw edges together with a 1/4-inch seam allowance. Center the seam on the backside of the sleeve; press. The raw edges of the seam will be concealed when the sleeve is stitched to the back of the quilt. Turn under both of the short raw edges; press and stitch to hem the ends. The final measurement should be about 1/2 inch from the quilt edges.

Pin the sleeve to the back of the quilt so the top edge of the sleeve is just below the binding. Hand-stitch the top edge of the sleeve in place, then the bottom edge. Make sure to knot and secure your stitches at each end of the sleeve to make sure it will not pull away from the quilt with use. Slip the rod into the casing. If your wall quilt is not directional, making a sleeve for the bottom edge will allow you to turn your quilt end to end to relieve the stress at the top edge. You could also slip a dowel into the bottom sleeve to help anchor the lower edge of the wall quilt.

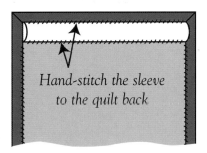

Hand-stitch the sleeve to the quilt back

Choosing a Quilt Design

Quilting is such an individual process that it is difficult to recommend designs for each quilt. There are hundreds of quilting stencils available at quilt shops. (Templates are used generally for appliqué shapes; stencils are used for marking quilting designs.)

There are a few suggestions that may help you decide how to quilt your project, depending on how much time you would like to spend quilting. Many quilters now use professional long-arm quilting machines or hire someone skilled at running these machines to do the quilting. This, of course, frees up more time to piece.

Quilting Suggestions

Repeat one of the design elements in the quilt as part of the quilting design.

Two or three parallel rows of echo quilting outside an appliqué piece will highlight the shape.

Stipple or meander quilting behind a feather or central motif will make the primary design more prominent.

Look for quilting designs that will cover two or more borders, rather than choosing separate designs for each individual border.

Quilting in the ditch of seams is an effective way to get a project quilted without a great deal of time marking the quilt.

Marking the Quilting Design

When marking the quilt top, use a marking tool that will be visible on the quilt fabric and yet will be easy enough to remove. Always test your marking tool on a scrap of fabric before marking the entire quilt.

Along with a multitude of commercial marking tools available, you may find that very thin slivers of hand soap (Dial, Ivory, etc.) work really well for marking medium to dark color fabrics. The thin lines of soap show up nicely and they are easily removed by simply rubbing gently with a piece of like-colored fabric.

Hints and Helps for Pressing Strip Sets

When sewing strips of fabric together for strip sets, it is important to press the seam allowances nice and flat, usually to the darker fabric. Be careful not to stretch as you press, causing a "rainbow effect." This will affect the accuracy and shape of the pieces cut from the strip set. I like to press on the wrong side first and with the strips perpendicular to the ironing board. Then I flip the piece over and press on the right side to prevent little pleats from forming at the seams. Laying the strip set lengthwise on the ironing board seems to encourage the rainbow effect, as shown in the diagram.

Avoid this rainbow effect

Borders

NOTE: Cut borders to the width called for. Always cut border strips a few inches longer than needed, just to be safe. Diagonally piece the border strips together as needed.

1. With pins, mark the center points along all 4 sides of the quilt. For the top and bottom borders, measure the quilt from left to right through the middle.

2. Measure and mark the border lengths and center points on the strips cut for the borders before sewing them on.

3. Pin the border strips to the quilt and stitch a 1/4-inch seam. Press the seam allowances toward the border. Trim off excess border lengths.

    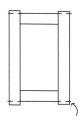

    Trim away excess fabric

4. For the side borders, measure your quilt from top to bottom, including the borders just added, to determine the length of the side borders.

5. Measure and mark the side border lengths as you did for the top and bottom borders.

6. Pin and stitch the side border strips in place. Press and trim the border strips even with the borders just added.

    Trim away excess fabric

7. If your quilt has multiple borders, measure, mark, and sew additional borders to the quilt in the same manner.

Decorative Stitches

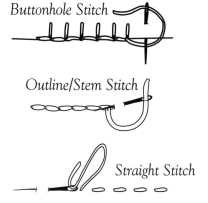

Buttonhole Stitch

Outline/Stem Stitch

Straight Stitch

Finishing the Quilt

1. Remove the selvages from the backing fabric. Sew the long edges together, and press. Trim the backing and batting so they are 2 inches to 4 inches larger than the quilt top.

2. Mark the quilt top for quilting. Layer the backing, batting, and quilt top. Baste the 3 layers together and quilt.

3. When quilting is complete, remove basting. Hand-baste all 3 layers together a scant 1/4 inch from the edge. This hand-basting keeps the layers from shifting and prevents puckers from forming when adding the binding. Trim excess batting and backing fabric even with the edge of the quilt top. Add the binding as shown below.

Binding and Diagonal Piecing

Diagonal Piecing

Stitch diagonally   *Trim to 1/4-inch seam allowance*   *Press seam open*

1. Diagonally piece the binding strips. Fold the strip in half lengthwise, wrong sides together, and press.

Double-layer Binding

2. Unfold and trim one end at a 45° angle. Turn under the edge 1/4 inch and press. Refold the strip.

Fold line

3. With raw edges of the binding and quilt top even, stitch with a 3/8-inch seam allowance, starting 2 inches from the angled end.

4. Miter the binding at the corners. As you approach a corner of the quilt, stop sewing 3/8 inch from the corner of the quilt.

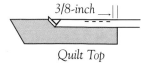

3/8-inch

Quilt Top

5. Clip the threads and remove the quilt from under the presser foot. Flip the binding strip up and away from the quilt, then fold the binding down even with the raw edge of the quilt. Begin sewing at the upper edge. Miter all 4 corners in this manner.

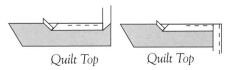

Quilt Top   *Quilt Top*

6. Trim the end of the binding so it can be tucked inside of the beginning binding about 3/8 inch. Finish stitching the seam.

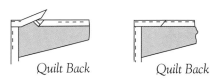

Quilt Back   *Quilt Back*

7. Turn the folded edge of the binding over the raw edges and to the back of the quilt so that the stitching line does not show. Hand-sew the binding in place, folding in the mitered corners as you stitch.

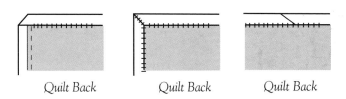

Quilt Back   *Quilt Back*   *Quilt Back*

SWATCHES TO GO

Lynette has created a palette of coordinating fabric
and color chips that blends perfectly for each season to
transition you through the year in style.

To use this practical system as the basis for your own
country decorating, simply take the page at right with four
seasons of "swatches to go" to your quilt shop or fabric store for
handy reference. The Thimbleberries® fabrics shown here are some
of Lynette's all-time favorites and may or may not be
currently available. However, the unique feature of
Thimbleberries® is that you can mix and match fabrics
because they blend from collection to collection. You'll find the
basic color palette an easy reference for selecting seasonal-color
fabric for quilts, pillows, and other decorating accessories.

Once you have selected your fabrics take them to your
paint store to choose complementary paint colors
for walls, painted furniture and accessories.

Thanks to Lynette, you can make it beautiful and make it
easy, too. With this unique system of "swatches to go" she
offers you the best of everything for creating four seasons
of your own authentic country decorating.

Spring

Summer

Harvest

Holiday

SOURCES

Many of Lynette Jensen's designs for quilts, pillows, and table runners shown in CLASSIC COUNTRY EXPANDED EDITION as decorative accessories are featured projects available from her Thimbleberries® line of books and patterns or from Rodale Books. Please call 800/587-3944 to order a catalog or for more information on obtaining patterns and instructions for the projects sourced in the gallery below.